ASIA BOND MONITOR
SEPTEMBER 2023

ASIAN DEVELOPMENT BANK

ADB

ISBN 978-92-9270-313-4 (print); 978-92-9270-314-1 (electronic); 978-92-9270-315-8 (ebook)
ISSN 2219-1518 (print), 2219-1526 (electronic)
Publication Stock No. TCS230340-2
DOI: http://dx.doi.org/10.22617/TCS230340-2

Note:
ADB recognizes "China" as the People's Republic of China; "Hong Kong" as Hong Kong, China; "Korea" as the Republic of Korea; "Siam" as Thailand; "Vietnam" as Viet Nam; and "Russia" as the Russian Federation.

Cover design by Erickson Mercado.

Contents

Emerging East Asian Local Currency Bond Markets: A Regional Update

Executive Summary

Recent Developments in Financial Conditions in Emerging East Asia

Financial conditions marginally improved between 1 June and 31 August in emerging East Asia on sound economic fundamentals and regional monetary tightening cycles approaching their end.[1] Most regional central banks kept their interest rate hikes on hold amid easing inflation, while some central banks started to lower rates to boost economic growth.

Most emerging East Asian economies witnessed narrowing risk premiums, gains in equity markets, and net foreign inflows in their bond markets. During the review period between 1 June and 31 August, regional markets excluding the People's Republic of China (PRC), where domestic financial markets weakened on a dimmed economic outlook, posted a market-weighted average gain of 1.4% in equity markets and a gross-domestic-product-weighted decline of 1.2 basis points in risk premiums, as captured by credit default swap spreads. Regional bond markets posted net foreign inflows of USD18.5 billion from April to July, partly supported by weakening inflation across the region. A dimmed economic outlook has softened investment sentiment in the PRC. Weighed down by this, regional equity markets posted net portfolio outflows of USD7.2 billion during the review period, largely driven by USD12.3 billion of net outflows from the PRC in August.

Regional currencies slightly weakened versus the United States (US) dollar amid ongoing monetary tightening and the positive economic outlook in the US. During the review period, regional currencies slightly depreciated against the dollar by 1.5% (simple average) and 1.9% (gross-domestic-product-weighted average).

From 1 June to 31 August, local currency (LCY) government bond yields rose in most emerging East Asian markets, following rising bond yields in major advanced economies. Only yields in the PRC and Viet Nam declined, as their respective central banks cut policy rates to support economic activities and safeguard financial stability.

The risk outlook for regional financial conditions is generally balanced. On the upside, softening inflation in the region has led most regional central banks to move toward the end of their monetary tightening cycles. A faster-than-expected decline in inflation in advanced economies, combined with financial risk considerations, might lead to a less hawkish monetary stance in advanced economies. However, the inflation path remains uncertain. Elevated price pressures together with a robust economic performance and strong job market in the US could support further monetary tightening.

On the downside, higher interest rates could challenge regional public and private borrowers with vulnerable balance sheets and weak governance. The Asian banking sector demonstrated its resilience amid the banking turmoil in the US and Europe earlier this year and the ratings downgrade of 10 mid-sized US banks in August. However, vulnerabilities have been present among both public and private sector borrowers since 2022, due to rising borrowing costs and tightened financial conditions. The Lao People's Democratic Republic has been rated by the International Monetary Fund as being "in debt distress" for both external and public debt, with public debt being deemed "unsustainable." Cambodia recorded a rising share of nonperforming loans in 2022, and some regional economies' corporate bond markets have experienced defaults in recent months. For example, the PRC and Viet Nam witnessed corporate bond defaults, especially in the real estate sector, while in Thailand, weak governance has been noted as a contributing factor in some cases of default. Headwinds to the regional economic outlook can also challenge financial conditions, as high interest rates could dampen consumption and investment, and weakness in the PRC's property sector could affect the broader economy and negatively affect the regional economic outlook.

---

[1] Emerging East Asia is defined to include member states of the Association of Southeast Asian Nations (ASEAN) plus the People's Republic of China; Hong Kong, China; and the Republic of Korea.

Recent Developments in Local Currency Bond Markets in Emerging East Asia

By the end of the second quarter (Q2) of 2023, LCY bonds outstanding in emerging East Asia totaled USD23.1 trillion on growth of 2.0% quarter-on-quarter (q-o-q). Growth in government bonds outstanding eased to 2.3% q-o-q in Q2 2023 from 2.6% q-o-q in the prior quarter as many governments frontloaded bond issuance in the first quarter (Q1) of 2023. Regional corporate bonds outstanding also saw weaker growth of 1.4% q-o-q in Q2 2023, compared with 1.6% q-o-q in Q1 2023, over sizeable amounts of maturities in nearly all markets. Government bonds accounted for 62.0% of the region's total LCY bond stock at the end of June. Association of Southeast Asian Nations (ASEAN) markets comprised a collective share of 9.1% of the regional LCY bond total with aggregate LCY bonds outstanding of USD2.1 trillion at the end of June.

During Q2 2023, emerging East Asia's LCY bond issuance reached USD2.4 trillion—with growth moderating to 4.6% q-o-q from 6.2% q-o-q in Q1 2023. Government bonds issuance, which comprised 41.7% of regional total LCY bond issuance in Q2 2023, posted growth of 2.2% q-o-q, decelerating from 12.4% q-o-q in Q1 2023. The slowing growth was largely driven by some governments tapering their issuance volumes after frontloading financing needs in Q1 2023. On the other hand, corporate bond issuance rebounded during the quarter, surging 12.6% q-o-q in Q2 2023, following a 1.1% q-o-q contraction in Q1 2023, led by the PRC and the Republic of Korea. ASEAN markets' aggregate issuance during the quarter reached USD470.4 billion, accounting for 20.0% of the regional issuance total despite a 6.5% q-o-q contraction.

The region's Treasury bond markets are dominated by medium- to long-term financing. Treasury bonds with a maturity of more than 5 years accounted for 53.2% of regional Treasury bonds outstanding at the end of June and 54.8% of Treasury bond issuance during Q2 2023. The size-weighted average maturities of Treasury bonds outstanding and issued in Q2 2023 were 8.5 years and 6.7 years, respectively. Meanwhile, around 89% of regional LCY Treasury bonds were held by domestic investors at the end of June.

Sustainable bonds outstanding in ASEAN+3 reached USD694.4 billion at the end of June, growing 5.1% q-o-q and 31.5% year-on-year in Q2 2023.[2] The expansion of ASEAN+3 sustainable bonds outstanding was roughly in line with that of the global sustainable bond market (5.5% q-o-q). ASEAN+3 accounted for 19.1% of global sustainable bonds outstanding at the end of June, making it the second-largest regional sustainable bond market in the world following the European Union's (EU-20) 38.5% share. Nevertheless, ASEAN+3's sustainable bond market accounts for only 1.9% of ASEAN+3's overall bond market, which is much smaller than the corresponding share of 6.6% for the EU-20.

During Q2 2023, ASEAN+3 sustainable bond issuance totaled USD69.0 billion, growing 19.7% q-o-q after a contraction of 0.6% q-o-q in Q1 2023. LCY issuance accounted for 78.4% of ASEAN+3 sustainable bond issuance in Q2 2023. Moreover, ASEAN+3 sustainable bond issuance tended to be concentrated in relatively short-term financing, with 59.9% of issuance in Q2 2023 having a maturity of 3 years or less. ASEAN+3's size-weighted average tenor for sustainable bond issuance in Q2 2023 was 4.8 years, or about half of the EU-20's average of 9.1 years over the same period. Around 69.0% of ASEAN+3 sustainable bond issuance was from the private sector in Q2 2023, compared with 44.2% in the EU-20.

---

[2] ASEAN+3 is defined to include member states of the Association of Southeast Asian Nations (ASEAN) plus the People's Republic of China; Hong Kong, China; Japan; and the Republic of Korea.

Developments in Regional Financial Conditions

Improved economic fundamentals in emerging East Asia buoyed investor sentiment in the region.

Financial conditions marginally improved in emerging East Asia from 1 June to 31 August, supported by sound economic fundamentals and regional central banks approaching the end of their respective monetary tightening cycles.[1] As major advanced economies continued with monetary tightening to address inflation, bond yields in advanced economies rose, which pushed up bond yields in most emerging East Asian markets. During the review period from 1 June to 31 August, most regional economies witnessed narrowing risk premiums, gains in the equity markets, and portfolio inflows in the bond markets. Regional currencies slightly depreciated against the United States (US) dollar, as the dollar strengthened on a resilient economic outlook for the US and continued hawkishness by the Federal Reserve. A dimmed economic outlook in the People's Republic of China (PRC) weighed down its domestic financial markets. Looming financial

risks remain worth monitoring, as higher interest rates will challenge both public and private sector entities with weak balance sheets and governance. During the review period, debt stress and bond defaults were observed in some regional markets.

Government bond yields in the US rose from 1 June to 31 August, mainly supported by the continued monetary tightening of the Federal Reserve as well as elevated inflation and solid economic conditions (**Table A**). After three consecutive rate hikes in February, March, and May—for a total of 75 basis points (bps)—the Federal Reserve paused hiking rates at its 13–14 June Federal Open Market Committee (FOMC) meeting to reassess economic conditions and the possible effects of banking sector stress on credit availability. Citing elevated inflation and robust job gains, the Federal Reserve resumed with a 25 bps rate hike at the 25–26 July FOMC meeting, as was widely expected, raising the federal funds target rate to 5.25%–5.50%, the highest level since February 2001 (**Figure A**).

Table A: Changes in Financial Conditions in Major Advanced Economies and Select Emerging East Asian Markets from 1 June 2023 to 31 August 2023

	2-Year Government Bond Yield (bps)	10-Year Government Bond Yield (bps)	5-Year Credit Default Swap Spread (bps)	Equity Index (%)	FX Rate (%)
Major Advanced Economies					
Germany	26	22	3	0.6	0.8
Japan	9	23	2	8.9	(4.6)
United States	52	51	–	6.8	–
Select Emerging East Asian Markets					
China, People's Rep. of	(3)	(12)	10	(2.6)	(2.2)
Hong Kong, China	24	29	–	0.9	(0.2)
Indonesia	62	0.9	(5)	4.8	(1.6)
Korea, Rep. of	14	28	(6)	(0.5)	(0.1)
Malaysia	9	13	(12)	5.0	(0.5)
Philippines	33	55	(9)	(4.0)	(0.6)
Singapore	13	25	–	2.1	(0.3)
Thailand	20	27	(5)	2.9	(0.6)
Viet Nam	(80)	(54)	2	13.5	(2.5)

( ) = negative, – = not available, bps = basis points, FX = foreign exchange.

Note: A positive (negative) value for the FX rate indicates the appreciation (depreciation) of the local currency against the United States dollar.

Source: *AsianBondsOnline* calculations based on Bloomberg LP data.

---

[1] Emerging East Asia is defined to include member states of the Association of Southeast Asian Nations (ASEAN) plus the People's Republic of China; Hong Kong, China; and the Republic of Korea.

Figure A: Inflation and Federal Funds Target Rate in the United States

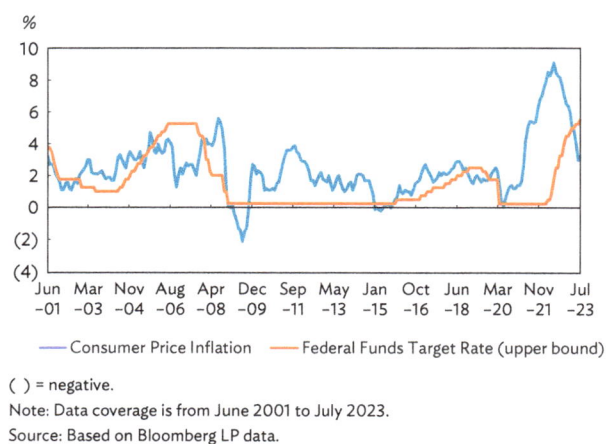

( ) = negative.
Note: Data coverage is from June 2001 to July 2023.
Source: Based on Bloomberg LP data.

In the US, bond yields increased during the review period, supported by elevated inflation and a positive economic outlook. The US economy grew an annualized 2.1% per the revised reading for the second quarter (Q2) of 2023, surpassing 2.0% growth in the previous quarter, driven by the rebound in private investment and increases in government expenditure and consumer spending. Consumer Price Index inflation has largely eased, falling from 4.0% year-on-year (y-o-y) in May to 3.0% y-o-y in June and 3.2% y-o-y in July. Core inflation, which excludes food and energy prices, moderated from 5.3% y-o-y in May to 4.8% y-o-y in June and 4.7% y-o-y in July. As inflation stayed well above the 2.0% target, the Federal Reserve remains hawkish. On 15 August, the Federal Reserve minutes showed that while participants noted inflation has trended downward, it is still "unacceptably" high. In line with this, Federal Reserve Chairman Jerome Powell, during the Jackson Hole Symposium on 25 August, said that while inflation has moved down from its peak, it is still too high.

The US labor market slightly softened but remained strong. The unemployment rate rose to 3.8% in August from 3.5% in July and 3.6% in June. Nonfarm payroll additions were lower in June (105,000), July (157,000), and August (187,000) compared to May (281,000). Average hourly earnings growth slowed to 0.2% month-on-month in August from 0.4% month-on-month in July and June. Easing inflation, a slight cooling in the job market, and the recent credit downgrade of 10 mid-sized

banks by Moody's after the FOMC July meeting have led to market expectations of a pause in rate hikes at the upcoming September meeting. The CME FedWatch Tool probability of a 25 bps rate hike at the September FOMC meeting decreased from 22.0% on 27 July, after the July FOMC meeting, to 12.0% on 31 August and 6.0% on 1 September.[2] At the Jackson Hole Symposium, Chairman Powell also indicated that the Federal Reserve would proceed carefully in the next few meetings, suggesting that a pause is likely in the September FOMC meeting.

In the euro area, both 2-year and 10-year bond yields increased on continued monetary tightening by the European Central Bank (ECB) and persistent inflationary pressures. In contrast to the Federal Reserve's pause, the ECB raised its key interest rate consecutively by 25 bps at its 15 June and 27 July meetings. Inflation in the euro area decelerated from 8.6% y-o-y in January to 6.1% y-o-y in May, then fell further to 5.5% y-o-y in June and 5.3% y-o-y in July. The flash estimate for August inflation was unchanged from the previous month at 5.3% y-o-y. The flash estimate for core inflation, however, weakened to 5.3% y-o-y in August from 5.5% y-o-y in July. The ECB has projected inflation in the euro area will remain elevated for some time as price pressures remain strong. Unlike in the US, the euro area's economic outlook remains weak. The near-term economic outlook for the euro area has deteriorated, owing largely to weaker domestic demand as high inflation and tighter financing conditions dampen spending. GDP growth in the euro area fell to 0.6% y-o-y in Q2 2023 from 1.1% y-o-y in the previous quarter. In June, the ECB revised downward its 2023 GDP forecast to 0.9% from its March forecast of 1.0%, while it revised upward its inflation forecast to 5.4% from 5.3% in the same period. The European Commission's monthly economic sentiment index fell to 93.3 in August from 94.5 in July, its fourth straight monthly decline. The weakening economic conditions are increasing the chance of a rate-hike pause at the September meeting, according to a poll of economists by Reuters published on 11 August. ECB Executive Board member Isabel Schnabel mentioned at a conference on 31 August that recent data suggested that the economic outlook had worsened compared to forecasts made in June. As a result, the implied probability of a rate hike at the September ECB meeting fell to 23.9% on 31 August from 54.6% the previous day, based on Bloomberg's World Interest Rate Probability

---

[2] CME FedWatch Tool.

for the euro area. Nevertheless, the future path of monetary tightening remains uncertain as ECB President Christine Lagarde previously implied in an interview on 28 July that any possible pause in September could still be followed by further rate hikes.

In Japan, despite inflation consistently exceeding the central bank's target and amid signs of economic recovery, the Bank of Japan (BOJ) maintained its accommodative monetary stance during the review period. Japan's inflation slowed from 3.5% y-o-y in April to 3.2% y-o-y in May before rising marginally to 3.3% y-o-y in June and July, remaining above the BOJ's 2.0% target. In its 15–16 June and 27–28 July meetings, the BOJ kept the short-term interest rate at –0.1% but raised its cap on 10-year government bond yields, through which it offers to purchase 10-year government bonds, to 1.0% from 0.5% set at its July meeting. This resulted in a jump in 10-year government bond yields to around 0.57% on 28 July, the highest level in nearly a decade, from 0.45% the previous day. The BOJ lowered Japan's 2023 GDP forecast to 1.3% in July from 1.4% in April and revised the inflation forecast for fiscal year 2023 to 2.5% in July from 1.8% in April. Meanwhile, Japan's GDP grew an annualized 6.0% in Q2 2023, up from 3.7% in the previous quarter, driven by strong export growth.

Most regional central banks paused and held interest rates at a high level during the review period after aggressive tightening in prior quarters (**Table B**). The region witnessed softening inflation during the past several months, which allowed most regional central banks to keep policy rate hikes on hold, with only the Bank of Thailand raising its policy rate by 25 bps on 2 August. The central bank expects the current positive economic trajectory to continue and is aiming to guard against potential inflationary pressures (**Figure B**).

Bond yields in most emerging East Asian markets continued to rise, partly following higher bond yields in major advanced economies (Table A). The Philippines experienced some of the region's largest increases in the 2-year and 10-year yields, with the 2-year tenor rising 33 bps and the 10-year rising 55 bps, driven by elevated inflation. July inflation in the Philippines remained high at 4.7% y-o-y, the highest in the region among markets where data are available. Both Viet Nam and the PRC experienced yield declines from 1 June to 31 August on monetary easing. Viet Nam recorded the region's largest decline in both the 2-year and 10-year bond yield at 80 bps and 54 bps, respectively, as the State Bank of Vietnam further cut its key policy rates by 50 bps in June—after two consecutive rate cuts

Table B: Changes in Monetary Stances in Major Advanced Economies and Select Emerging East Asian Markets

Economy	Policy Rate 1-Aug-2022 (%)	Rate Change (%) Aug-2022	Sep-2022	Oct-2022	Nov-2022	Dec-2022	Jan-2023	Feb-2023	Mar-2023	Apr-2023	May-2023	Jun-2023	Jul-2023	Aug-2023	Policy Rate 31-Aug-2023 (%)	Change in Policy Rates (basis points)
Euro Area	0.00		↑0.75		↑0.75	↑0.50		↑0.50	↑0.50		↑0.25	↑0.25		↑0.25	3.75	↑375
Japan	(0.10)														(0.10)	0
United Kingdom	1.25	↑0.50	↑0.50		↑0.75	↑0.50		↑0.50	↑0.25		↑0.25	↑0.50		↑0.25	5.25	↑400
United States	2.50		↑0.75		↑0.75	↑0.50		↑0.25	↑0.25		↑0.25		↑0.25		5.50	↑300
China, People's Rep. of	2.85	↓0.10										↓0.10		↓0.15	2.50	↓35
Indonesia	3.50	↑0.25	↑0.50	↑0.50	↑0.50	↑0.25	↑0.25								5.75	↑225
Korea, Rep. of	2.25	↑0.25		↑0.50	↑0.25		↑0.25								3.50	↑125
Malaysia	2.25		↑0.25		↑0.25						↑0.25				3.00	↑75
Philippines	3.25	↑0.50	↑0.50		↑0.75	↑0.50		↑0.50	↑0.25						6.25	↑300
Singapore	–		↑												–	–
Thailand	0.50	↑0.25	↑0.25		↑0.25		↑0.25		↑0.25		↑0.25			↑0.25	2.25	↑175
Viet Nam	4.00		↑1.00	↑1.00					↓0.50	↓0.50		↓0.50			4.50	↑50

( ) = negative, – = no data.

Notes:
1. Data coverage is from 1 August 2022 to 31 August 2023.
2. For the People's Republic of China, data used in the chart are for the 1-year medium-term lending facility rate. While the 1-year benchmark lending rate is the official policy rate of the People's Bank of China, market players use the 1-year medium-term lending facility rate as a guide for the monetary policy direction of the People's Bank of China.
3. The up (down) arrow for Singapore signifies monetary policy tightening (loosening) by its central bank. The Monetary Authority of Singapore utilizes the Singapore dollar nominal effective exchange rate to guide its monetary policy.

Sources: Various central bank websites.

Figure B: Inflation in Advanced and Select Emerging East Asian Economies

%, y-o-y

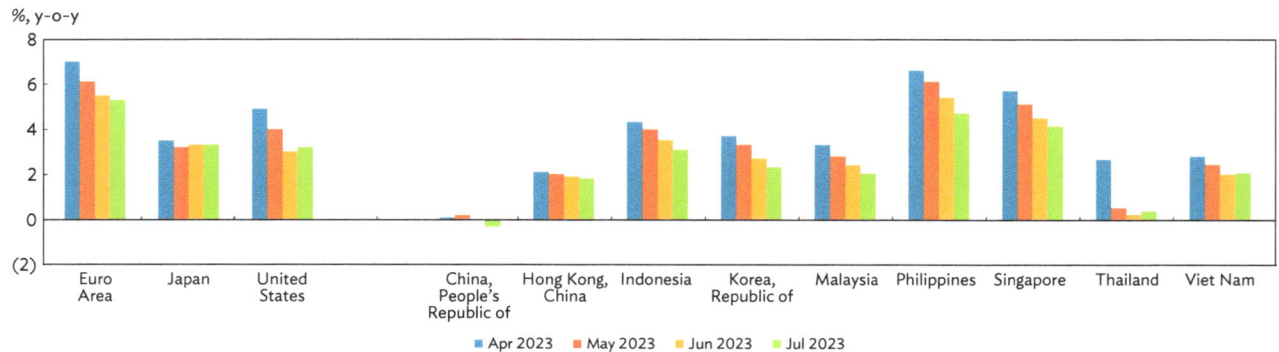

Apr 2023 May 2023 Jun 2023 Jul 2023

y-o-y = year-on-year.
Notes:
1. Data coverage is from April to July 2023.
2. For the People's Republic of China, inflation for April and June 2023 were 0.1% y-o-y and 0.0% y-o-y, respectively.
Sources: Various local sources.

of 50 bps each in April and May—to boost economic growth. Both the 2-year (3 bps) and 10-year (12 bps) yield fell in the PRC during the review period. In June, the People's Bank of China reduced several key interest rates, including the medium-term lending facility and the loan prime rate, by 10 bps each to boost economic activities. In August, the PRC reduced the 1-year medium-term lending facility rate by 15 bps and the 7-day reverse repo and 1-year loan prime rate by 10 bps each.

A hawkish Federal Reserve and the sound economic outlook in the US led to the dollar strengthening against most regional currencies. During the review period, regional currencies posted a slight depreciation of 1.5% (simple average) and 1.9% (GDP-weighted) (**Figure C**). Excluding the Chinese yuan, regional currencies only marginally depreciated versus the US dollar by 1.4% (simple average) and 0.8% (GDP-weighted average). Among regional currencies, the Laotian kip experienced the most significant depreciation of 8.5%, weighed down by negative investor sentiment over debt stress and elevated inflation. The Chinese yuan weakened over heightened concerns regarding the PRC's economic outlook.

Box 1 discusses how global shocks affect the real economy in emerging East Asia through exchange rates.

Despite the slightly stronger US dollar, softening inflationary pressures and sound economic fundamentals boosted investment sentiment in most regional markets.

Figure C: Changes in Select Emerging East Asian Currencies versus the United States Dollar

%

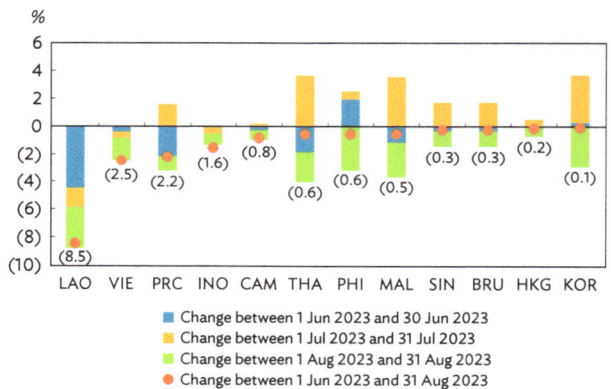

- Change between 1 Jun 2023 and 30 Jun 2023
- Change between 1 Jul 2023 and 31 Jul 2023
- Change between 1 Aug 2023 and 31 Aug 2023
- Change between 1 Jun 2023 and 31 Aug 2023

( ) = negative; BRU = Brunei Darussalam; CAM = Cambodia; HKG = Hong Kong, China; INO = Indonesia; KOR = Republic of Korea; LAO = Lao People's Democratic Republic; MAL = Malaysia; PHI = Philippines; PRC = People's Republic of China; SIN = Singapore; THA = Thailand; VIE = Viet Nam.
Notes:
1. A positive (negative) value for the foreign exchange rate indicates the appreciation (depreciation) of the local currency against the United States dollar.
2. The numbers above (below) each bar refer to the change between 1 June 2023 and 31 August 2023.
Source: *AsianBondsOnline* calculations based on Bloomberg LP data.

Equity markets gained in a majority of regional economies during the review period. Excluding the PRC, equity markets in the region gained a market-weighted average of 1.4%. However, the regional average was weighed down by equity market losses in the PRC in August, with the region's equity market performance during the review period recording a market-weighted average

Box 1: Global Shocks and Exchange Rate Pass-Through in Emerging Asia

Over the past 25 years, central banks in emerging Asia have improved their monetary policy frameworks, helping to anchor inflation expectations and support broader macroeconomic stability.[a] While this has also contributed to enhancing the resilience of Asian economies to external shocks, the exchange rate channel remains a key transmission mechanism of disturbances to the real economy and financial markets.

During 2022, aggressive United States (US) monetary policy tightening in the face of soaring inflation triggered exchange-rate-driven inflationary pressures at the global level, with the US dollar appreciating to levels not observed in decades. Given the US dollar pricing of international commodities, net commodity importers during this period experienced sharp currency depreciations and imported inflation. Central banks therefore need to pay close attention to exchange rate developments that might affect their price stability mandates.

Since most developing economies depend on foreign currency for engaging in international trade, their exchange rate pass-through (ERPT) elasticity can be subject to significant variations related to the sectoral composition of the economy and exposure to external economic and financial developments (Burstein and Gopinath 2014; Forbes, Hjortsoe, and Nenova 2018). In addition, given rising levels of global financial integration, emerging market economies (EMEs) are vulnerable to global financial shocks and monetary spillovers, notably via the exchange rate channel (Han and Wei 2018). A new Asian Development Bank Institute paper by Beirne, Renzhi, and Panthi (2023) examines the evolution of ERPT to prices for emerging economies in Asia. Time-varying estimates of ERPT reveal that it has been declining for most Asian EMEs since around 2010, which corresponds to the period after the global financial crisis. **Figure B1.1** shows the estimates relative to consumer prices.

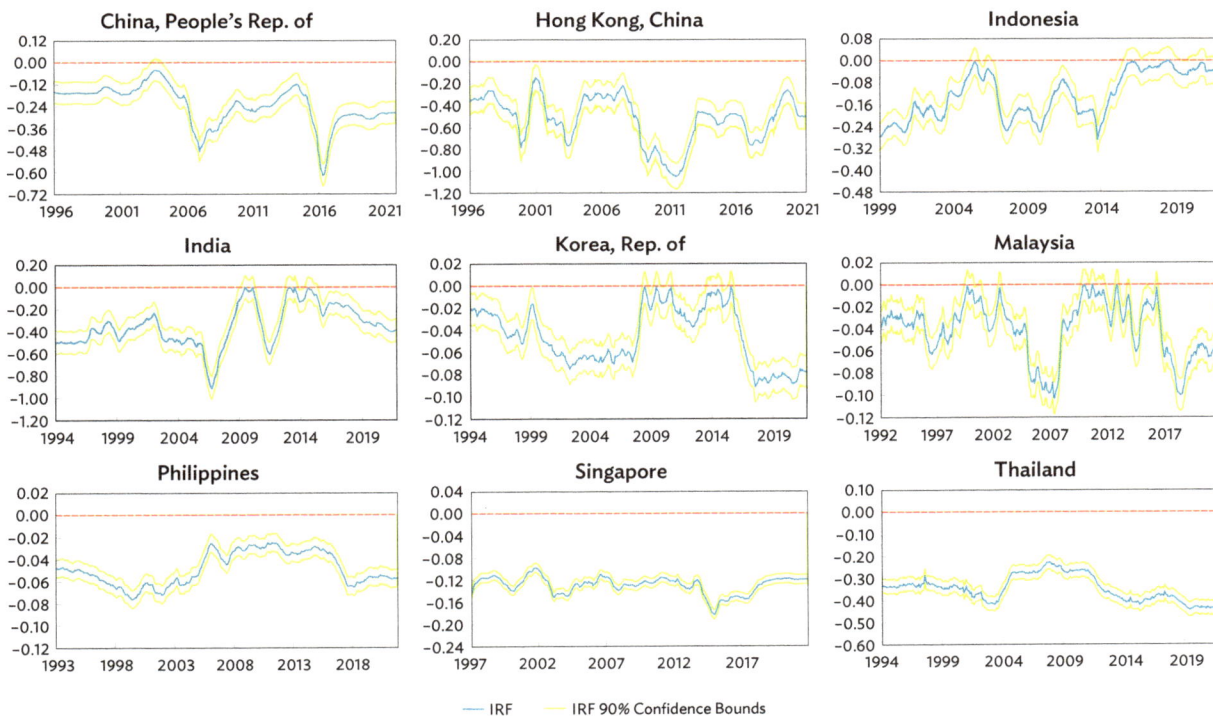

Figure B1.1: Time-Varying Exchange Rate Pass-Through to Consumer Prices

IRF = impulse response function.

Notes: The figure plots yearly time-varying impulse responses of consumer prices to a 1 percentage point appreciation shock of the exchange rate, with 90% confidence intervals. The vertical axis unit is percentage points, and the unit of the horizontal axis refers to months.

Source: Beirne, Renzhi, and Panthi (2023).

---

[a] This box was written by John Beirne (vice-chair of research and senior research fellow) of the Asian Development Bank Institute in Tokyo; Nuobu Renzhi (assistant professor) at the School of Economics of Capital University of Economics and Business in Beijing; and Pradeep Panthi (research associate) of the Asian Development Bank Institute in Tokyo.

continued on next page

Box 1   *continued*

During the post-global-financial-crisis period, Asian economies significantly enhanced their overall macrofinancial resilience capacities, supported by improved central bank credibility. Nonetheless, Asian EMEs continue to remain vulnerable to external real and financial shocks, albeit to differing degrees depending on the nature of the shock. Beirne, Renzhi, and Panthi (2023) also show that ERPT is incomplete and mostly higher for producer than consumer prices and mostly greater in magnitude over a longer horizon of 12 months.

Regarding the significance of global shocks, the authors find that oil price and global output shocks mostly affect longer-term producer price ERPT in emerging Asia, while US monetary policy and global financial market volatility shocks mostly affect longer-term consumer price ERPT in emerging Asia. The response of ERPT to consumer prices due to US monetary policy tightening shocks is shown in **Figure B1.2**. While some heterogeneity is found in the magnitude and duration of statistical significance, US monetary policy tightening shocks amplify ERPT to consumer prices in emerging Asia in most cases, with the results most pronounced over the longer-term horizon.

Policy Implications for Central Banks in Emerging Asia

While ERPT has in general trended downward and varies somewhat across economies in terms of its elasticity, it has a material and statistically significant effect on inflation, with evidence of persistence. This implies that exchange rate developments are important considerations for central banks in the sense that they can affect their core mandates for price stability. While recognizing the shock-absorbing capacity of exchange rates in flexible exchange rate regime settings, a persistently high rate of ERPT could trigger an assessment of the appropriateness of the monetary policy framework.

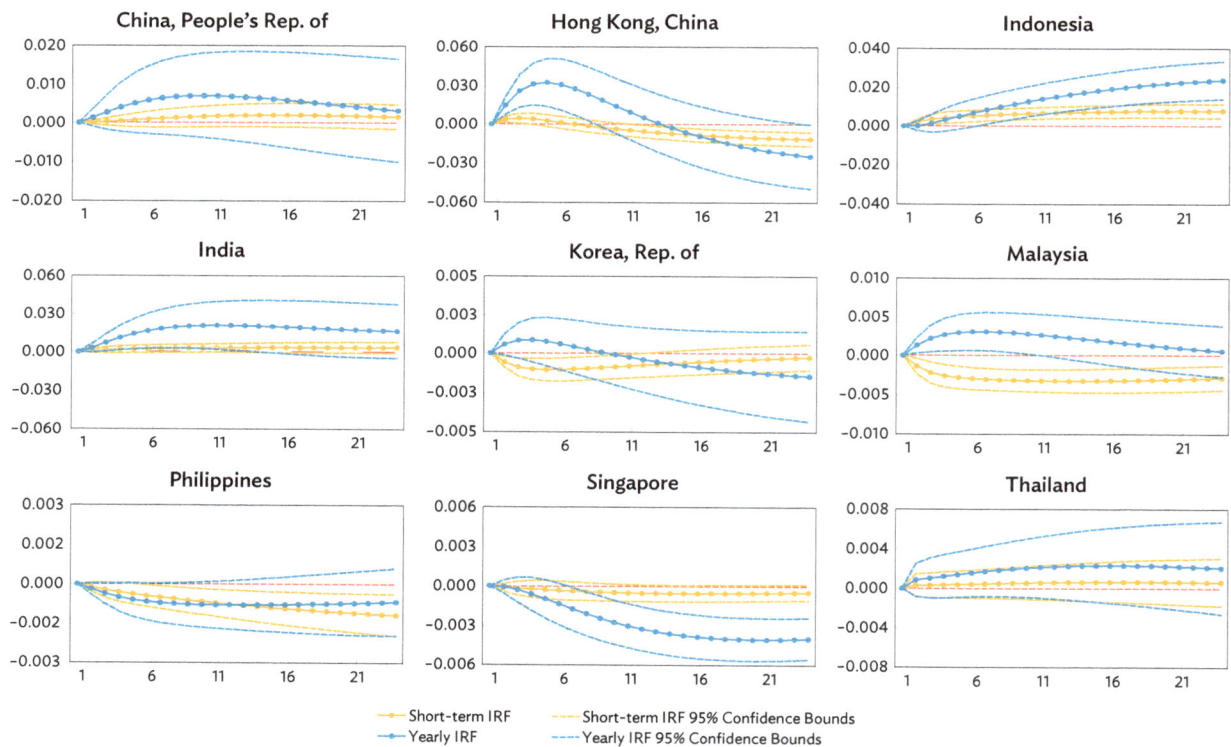

Figure B1.2: United States Monetary Policy Shocks and the Response of Exchange Rate Pass-Through to Consumer Prices

IRF = impulse response function.

Notes: Impulse responses with 95% confidence bands are reported. Yellow lines refer to the short-term exchange rate pass-through and blue lines refer to the yearly exchange rate pass-through. The vertical axis unit is percentage points, and the unit of the horizontal axis refers to months.

Source: Beirne, Renzhi, and Panthi (2023).

continued on next page

Box 1 *continued*

The findings from the paper also have implications for policy makers and central banks in shielding their economies from the ERPT effects of global economic and financial shocks. For example, amplified ERPT to producer prices from oil price shocks could trigger an acceleration of efforts aimed at reducing concentration risks through the diversification of energy supply networks. For central banks, the dominant role of US monetary policy in driving the global financial cycle makes it a difficult proposition for emerging Asian economies to have buffers in place against US monetary policy shocks. However, strong macroeconomic fundamentals are an important consideration in this regard, including adequate foreign exchange reserve accumulation.

Finally, these results can also help central banks to improve forecasts of inflation that derive from exchange rate movements. While fraught with difficulty and notoriously bound by wide margins of error, the lags in monetary policy in affecting inflation mean that accuracy in inflation forecasting is central to effective monetary policy. The incorporation of time-varying ERPT estimates into inflation forecasting models may be an area worth further examination.

References

Beirne, John, Nuobu Renzhi, and Pradeep Panthi. 2023. Exchange Rate Pass-Through in Emerging Asia and Exposure to External Shocks. ADBI Working Papers No. 1379.

Burstein, Ariel, and Gita Gopinath. 2014. International Prices and Exchange Rates. In *Handbook of International Economics*, edited by Gita Gopinath, Elhanan Helpman, and Kenneth Rogoff, pp. 391–451. Amsterdam: Elsevier.

Forbes, Kristin, Ida Hjortsoe, and Tsvetelina Nenova. 2018. The Shocks Matter: Improving Our Estimates of Exchange Rate Pass-Through. *Journal of International Economics* 114 (C): 255–75.

Han, Xuehui, and Shang-Jin Wei. 2018. International Transmissions of Monetary Shocks: Between a Trilemma and a Dilemma. *Journal of International Economics* 110 (C): 205–19.

decline of 0.9%. Investment sentiment in regional equity markets was significantly boosted in July when the PRC announced additional policy support to stimulate its economy, but it weakened following a series of negative economic news in August (**Figure D**). Investor risk aversion rose following Fitch's downgrade of the sovereign credit rating of the US on 1 August and Moody's downgrade of the credit ratings of 10 mid-sized US banks on 7 August. Risk aversion was further exacerbated when the PRC reported negative export growth for July on 8 August and a decline in July consumer prices on 9 August. On 10 August, the US announced that it would restrict investments by US venture capital firms, private equity firms, and joint ventures in PRC companies involved in artificial intelligence, quantum computing, and semiconductors.

Similarly, improved risk sentiment during the review period pushed down risk premiums, which are typically reflected in the credit default swap spread, in most regional markets. During the review period, credit default swap spreads in the region excluding the PRC declined by 6.0 bps (simple average) and 1.2 bps

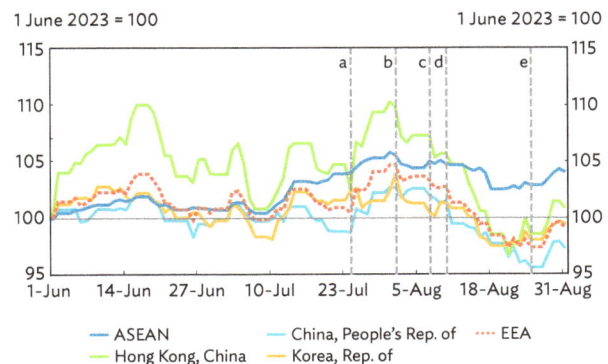

Figure D: Movements in Equity Indexes in Select Emerging East Asian Markets

1 June 2023 = 100   1 June 2023 = 100

ASEAN = Association of Southeast Asian Nations, EEA = emerging East Asia, PRC = People's Republic of China, US = United States.

a   The Government of the PRC promises additional economic support.
b   Fitch downgrades US' credit rating.
c   Moody's downgrades the credit ratings of 10 US banks.
d   US passes laws limiting PRC investments by US venture capital firms, private equity firms, and joint ventures.
e   US Fed chair Powell speaks at Jackson Hole.

Notes:
1.   ASEAN comprises the markets of Cambodia, Indonesia, the Lao People's Democratic Republic, Malaysia, the Philippines, Singapore, Thailand, and Viet Nam.
2.   Data are as of 31 August 2023.

Source: *AsianBondsOnline* calculations based on Bloomberg LP data.

Figure E: Changes in Credit Default Swap Spreads in Select Emerging East Asian Markets (senior 5-year)

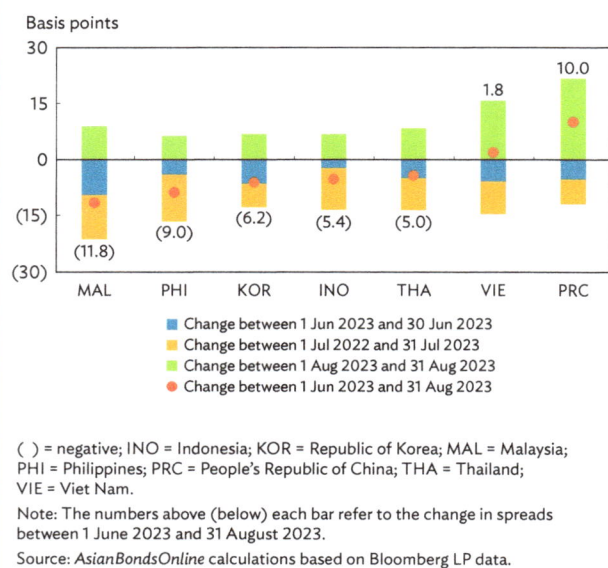

Basis points

- Change between 1 Jun 2023 and 30 Jun 2023
- Change between 1 Jul 2022 and 31 Jul 2023
- Change between 1 Aug 2023 and 31 Aug 2023
- Change between 1 Jun 2023 and 31 Aug 2023

( ) = negative; INO = Indonesia; KOR = Republic of Korea; MAL = Malaysia; PHI = Philippines; PRC = People's Republic of China; THA = Thailand; VIE = Viet Nam.
Note: The numbers above (below) each bar refer to the change in spreads between 1 June 2023 and 31 August 2023.
Source: *AsianBondsOnline* calculations based on Bloomberg LP data.

Figure F: Capital Flows in Equity Markets in Emerging East Asia

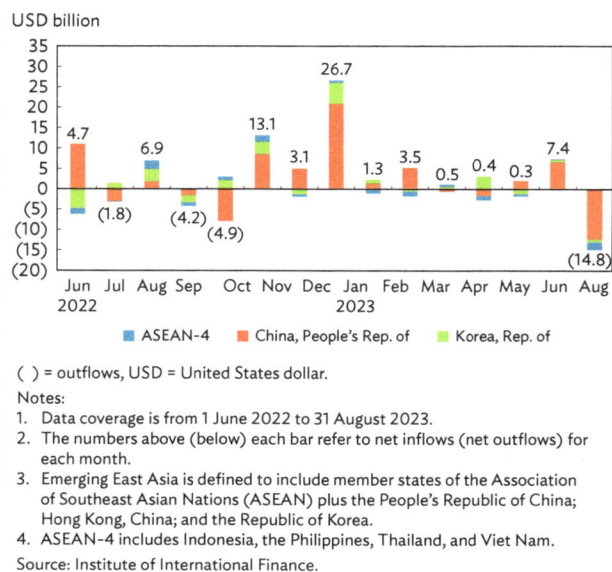

USD billion

- ASEAN-4
- China, People's Rep. of
- Korea, Rep. of

( ) = outflows, USD = United States dollar.
Notes:
1. Data coverage is from 1 June 2022 to 31 August 2023.
2. The numbers above (below) each bar refer to net inflows (net outflows) for each month.
3. Emerging East Asia is defined to include member states of the Association of Southeast Asian Nations (ASEAN) plus the People's Republic of China; Hong Kong, China; and the Republic of Korea.
4. ASEAN-4 includes Indonesia, the Philippines, Thailand, and Viet Nam.
Source: Institute of International Finance.

(GDP-weighted average). However, regional risk premiums widened by 6.8 bps (GDP-weighted average) if the PRC is included—due to its dimmed economic outlook (**Figure E**). The updated regional economic outlook can be found in the forthcoming September 2023 *Asian Development Outlook* report.

Between 1 June and 31 August, the region's equity markets posted combined net portfolio outflows of USD7.2 billion, driven largely by outflows of USD14.8 billion in August (**Figure F**). In June, regional equity markets posted minimal net foreign inflows, as the USD2.0 billion of net inflows to the PRC were offset by outflows from the Republic of Korea and member economies of the Association of Southeast Asian Nations (ASEAN). The Republic of Korea recorded net foreign capital outflows of USD1.3 billion in June following its failed bid to be included in MSCI's developed markets index despite a series of financial market reforms. ASEAN economies recorded net foreign outflows of USD0.5 billion in June on outflows from Indonesia (USD0.3 billion), Thailand (USD0.3 billion), and Viet Nam (USD0.02 billion). In both Indonesia and Viet Nam, the outflows were driven by a weakening export performance, while in Thailand the outflows were due to uncertainties in the political outlook. In July, regional markets recorded USD7.4 billion of net foreign inflows on improved sentiment over a possible pause in US rate hikes in September and the stimulus measures introduced in the PRC. However, a series of

negative news in August, especially the PRC's weak economic outlook, heightened risk aversion and drove portfolio outflows across the region. Emerging East Asian markets posted net outflows of USD14.8 billion in August, with the PRC recording the largest net foreign portfolio outflows of USD12.3 billion.

Elevated inflation in advanced economies led to net portfolio inflows of USD18.5 billion in the region's bond markets from April to July 2023. Net inflows of USD7.1 billion were recorded in June, following consecutive net inflows recorded in April (USD1.7 billion) and May (USD10.6 billion) (**Figure G**). Softening inflation in most emerging East Asian markets relative to the persistent elevated inflation in advanced economies partly contributed to the net inflows. The inflows were also influenced by a pause in tightening by the Federal Reserve in June. The Republic of Korea recorded the largest net bond inflows in the region in Q2 2023 at USD13.8 billion, followed by Malaysia (USD2.2 billion). ASEAN markets posted aggregate net inflows of USD2.4 billion in June, following net inflows of USD1.7 billion in May and net outflows of USD0.4 billion in April. Among ASEAN markets, Indonesia (USD1.9 billion) and Malaysia recorded net inflows in Q2 2023 due to relatively attractive yields compared with US Treasuries and easing inflation in both markets. In contrast, Thailand, recorded net outflows of USD0.2 billion due to political uncertainties following the general election in May.

Figure G: Foreign Capital Flows in Select Emerging East Asian Local Currency Bond Markets

USD billion

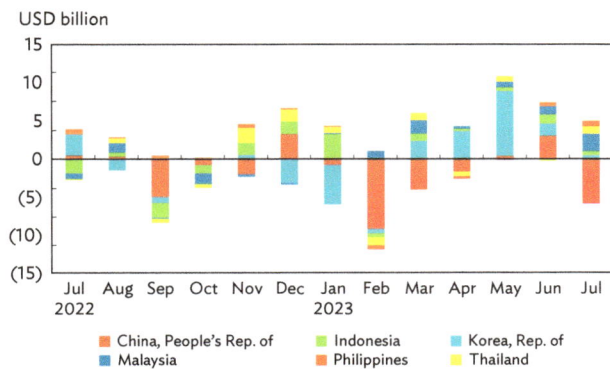

( ) = negative, USD = United States dollar.

Notes:
1. The Republic of Korea and Thailand provided data on bond flows. For the People's Republic of China, Indonesia, Malaysia, and the Philippines, month-on-month changes in foreign holdings of local currency government bonds were used as a proxy for bond flows.
2. Data are as of 31 July 2023.
3. Figures were computed based on 31 July 2023 exchange rates and do not include currency effects.

Sources: People's Republic of China (Bloomberg LP); Indonesia (Directorate General of Budget Financing and Risk Management, Ministry of Finance); Republic of Korea (Financial Supervisory Service); Malaysia (Bank Negara Malaysia); Philippines (Bureau of the Treasury); and Thailand (Thai Bond Market Association).

The Philippines also posted net marginal outflows of USD0.04 billion on relatively elevated inflation compared with other ASEAN economies. In July, however, weighed down by the PRC's weak economic outlook and lower interest rates, net foreign portfolio outflows of USD0.9 billion were observed in regional bond markets with USD5.9 billion of outflows from the PRC's bond market. All other regional bond markets recorded net inflows in July.

The risk outlook to regional financial conditions remains balanced. On the upside, softened inflation across the region led to a pause in monetary tightening by most regional central banks. Faster-than-expected declines in inflation in advanced economies, combined with financial risk and economic growth concerns, could lead to less hawkish monetary stances by major central banks such as the Federal Reserve and the ECB, further improving financial conditions in the region. However, different possible paces of disinflation have left uncertainty over the monetary policy directions of advanced economies. For example, sound economic growth and a strong labor market in the US combined with still-elevated inflation might support further tightening: On 15 August, Minneapolis Federal Reserve President

Neil Kashkari said he is still not ready to say that the Federal Reserve is done hiking rates. On 25 August, Federal Reserve Bank of Cleveland President Loretta Mester said that it was likely that the Federal Reserve would raise rates again and that work still needs to be done to bring inflation down.

Meanwhile, higher interest rates in both domestic and international markets have raised borrowing costs, challenging regional public and private borrowers with vulnerable balance sheets and weak governance. While Asian banks in general demonstrated resilience to negative banking sector news in advanced economies, such as turmoil in the US and European banking sectors earlier this year and the downgrade of 10 mid-sized US bank in August, regional public and private sector borrowers face similar higher debt burdens and interest risks (**Figure H**).

On the sovereign side, the Lao People's Democratic Republic (Lao PDR) has been assessed to be in "external and overall debt distress" by the International Monetary Fund's 2023 Article IV Consultation released in May 2023. Rating agencies have also been pessimistic dating back to last year. Moody's downgraded the Lao PDR's sovereign rating to Caa3 from Caa2 on 15 June 2022, and Fitch Ratings downgraded the Lao PDR's sovereign rating to CCC– from CCC on 4 August 2022 on rising external liquidity risks before subsequently withdrawing its ratings coverage on 10 October 2022.

Figure H: S&P Broad Market Indexes for Banking Stocks in Asia, Europe, and the United States

1 March 2023 = 100   1 March 2023 = 100

Notes:
1. Data are as of 31 August 2023.
2. S&P Global's Broad Market Indexes for banks are comprehensive benchmarks of bank stocks in Asia and the Pacific, Europe, and the United States, and are subindexes of the S&P Global BMI for Banks.

Source: S&P Global.

In the region's private sector, signs of vulnerability have appeared in the banking sector and in bond markets. In Cambodia, the banking sector witnessed an uptick in nonperforming loans in 2022. The ratio of nonperforming loans as a percentage of total loans in Cambodia's overall banking sector rose to 3.1% in 2022 from 2.0% in 2021, according to the National Bank of Cambodia's Annual Supervision Report 2022. In recent months, bond defaults have been observed in some regional bond corporate bond markets.

In the PRC, an S&P Global Ratings report in April 2023 estimated that the value of offshore defaults rose to USD54.0 billion in 2022 from USD10.0 billion in 2021, with the increase mostly coming from real estate companies. In 2023, a number of real estate companies reported payment difficulties. For example, Sino-Ocean, a property company, announced on 2 August that it would delay the principal repayments of a bond by 30 days. On 22 August, Sino-Ocean announced that it had reached an agreement with bond holders to delay repayment until August 2024. Country Garden Holdings, another property company, missed a coupon payment on one of its US dollar bonds on 7 August and later announced that it would be discussing repayment plans with its creditors on 14 August. However, as of 31 August, Country Garden had yet to reach an agreement and had delayed the vote on its bond repayment terms twice. On 18 August, Evergrande Group filed for bankruptcy protection in the US. Negotiations for its offshore debt-restructuring plan are still ongoing.

Corporate bond defaults have been rising in Viet Nam, especially in the real estate sector. In February 2023, No Va Land Investment Group, Viet Nam's second-largest property company, announced that it would delay payment of a VND1.0 trillion note due on 12 February. In May 2023, FiinRatings said that 98 firms had missed payments from 17 April to 4 May amounting to VND128.5 trillion. A June FiinRatings report estimated that as of June 2023, the total value of bond defaults was 26.9% of total nonbank corporate bonds outstanding.

In Thailand, three companies reported bond defaults in the first half of 2023 according to the Bank of Thailand. While the defaults only comprised about 0.3% of total Thai corporate bonds outstanding, the Bank of Thailand is undertaking increased surveillance and monitoring of corporates' refinancing activities. In addition, accounting irregularities discovered in a special audit of Stark Corporation Public Company, which defaulted on two bonds on 2 June, have called attention to the need for strengthening corporate governance and transparency in Thailand.

Headwinds to the regional economic outlook are also challenging financial conditions. With most regional central banks holding interest rates steady, higher borrowing costs could negatively affect investment and consumption. Concerns over the PRC's recent economic data and a subdued real estate sector could also negatively affect the growth outlook in other regional economies.

Bond Market Developments in the Second Quarter of 2023

Section 1. Size and Composition

Local currency (LCY) bonds outstanding in emerging East Asia amounted to USD23.1 trillion at the end of June, rising 7.9% from a year earlier.[3] Annual growth in the emerging East Asian LCY bond market exceeded that of the United States (US) and the European Union 20 (EU-20), which expanded 7.1% and 4.7%, respectively. In terms of overall size at the end of June, the emerging East Asian LCY bond market was equivalent to 63.1% of the US bond market and 114.2% of the EU-20 market (**Figure 1**).

On a quarterly basis, growth in the emerging East Asian LCY bond market decelerated to 2.0% in the second quarter (Q2) of 2023 from 2.2% in the preceding quarter (Figure 2). The slower growth largely reflected a relatively high volume of maturities and moderated issuance of government bonds. Growth in Treasury and other government bonds eased to 2.3% quarter-on-quarter (q-o-q) in Q2 2023 from 2.6% q-o-q in the first quarter (Q1) as many regional governments had previously frontloaded bond issuance in the preceding quarter to support economic recovery or revised borrowing plans (**Table 1**). For example, the

Figure 1: Local Currency Bonds Outstanding in Emerging East Asia, the EU-20, and the United States

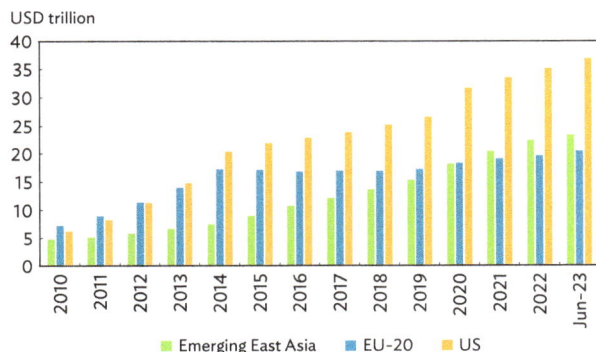

USD trillion

Legend: Emerging East Asia ■ EU-20 ■ US

EU = European Union, US = United States, USD = United States dollar.

Notes:
1. Emerging East Asia is defined to include the Association of Southeast Asian Nations plus the People's Republic of China; Hong Kong, China; and the Republic of Korea.
2. EU-20 includes EU member markets Austria, Belgium, Croatia, Cyprus, Estonia, Finland, France, Germany, Greece, Ireland, Italy, Latvia, Lithuania, Luxembourg, Malta, the Netherlands, Portugal, Slovakia, Slovenia, and Spain.

Sources: People's Republic of China (CEIC Data Company); Hong Kong, China (Hong Kong Monetary Authority); EU-20 (Bloomberg LP); Indonesia (Bank Indonesia; Directorate General of Budget Financing and Risk Management, Ministry of Finance; and Indonesia Stock Exchange); Republic of Korea (Bank of Korea and KG Zeroin Corporation); Malaysia (Bank Negara Malaysia); Philippines (Bureau of the Treasury and Bloomberg LP); Singapore (Monetary Authority of Singapore and Bloomberg LP); Thailand (Bank of Thailand); United States (Bloomberg LP); and Viet Nam (Bloomberg LP and Vietnam Bond Market Association).

Figure 2: Growth of Select Emerging East Asian Local Currency Bond Markets in the First and Second Quarters of 2023 (q-o-q, %)

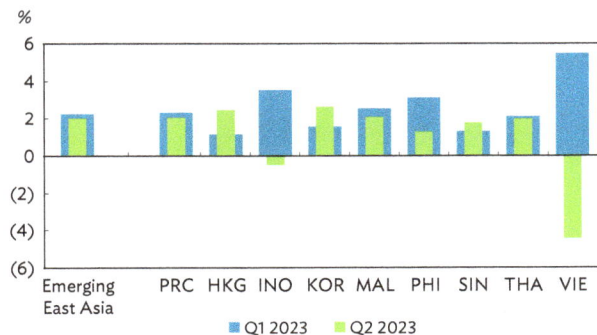

%

Legend: ■ Q1 2023 ■ Q2 2023

( ) = negative; HKG = Hong Kong, China; INO = Indonesia; KOR = Republic of Korea; MAL = Malaysia; PHI = Philippines; PRC = People's Republic of China; Q1 = first quarter; Q2 = second quarter; q-o-q = quarter-on-quarter; SIN = Singapore; THA = Thailand; VIE = Viet Nam.

Notes:
1. For Singapore, corporate bonds outstanding are based on *AsianBondsOnline* estimates.
2. Growth rates are calculated from a local currency base and do not include currency effects. For emerging East Asia, growth figures are based on 30 June 2023 currency exchange rates and do not include currency effects.

Sources: People's Republic of China (CEIC Data Company); Hong Kong, China (Hong Kong Monetary Authority); Indonesia (Bank Indonesia; Directorate General of Budget Financing and Risk Management, Ministry of Finance; and Indonesia Stock Exchange); Republic of Korea (Bank of Korea and KG Zeroin Corporation); Malaysia (Bank Negara Malaysia); Philippines (Bureau of the Treasury and Bloomberg LP); Singapore (Monetary Authority of Singapore and Bloomberg LP); Thailand (Bank of Thailand); and Viet Nam (Bloomberg LP and Vietnam Bond Market Association).

---

[3] Emerging East Asia is defined to include member states of the Association of Southeast Asian Nations (ASEAN) plus the People's Republic of China; Hong Kong, China; and the Republic of Korea.

Table 1: Size and Composition of Select Emerging East Asian Local Currency Bond Markets

	Q2 2022		Q1 2023		Q2 2023			Growth Rate (%) Q2 2023	
	Amount (USD billion)	% of GDP	Amount (USD billion)	% of GDP	Amount (USD billion)	% share	% of GDP	q-o-q	y-o-y
China, People's Rep. of									
Total	18,368	104.0	18,957	106.5	18,325	100.0	107.4	2.0	8.0
Treasury and Other Government	11,896	67.4	12,489	70.2	12,122	66.1	71.0	2.4	10.3
Central Bank	2	0.01	2	0.01	2	0.01	0.01	0.0	0.0
Corporate	6,469	36.6	6,465	36.3	6,201	33.8	36.3	1.2	3.8
Hong Kong, China									
Total	334	92.0	357	98.2	366	100.0	99.6	2.4	9.6
Treasury and Other Government	24	6.7	29	8.0	30	8.2	8.1	3.3	22.9
Government	152	41.8	155	42.6	157	43.0	42.6	0.9	3.1
Corporate	158	43.5	173	47.6	180	48.8	48.8	3.7	13.7
Indonesia									
Total	369	30.2	411	30.6	409	100.0	29.9	(0.5)	11.5
Treasury and Other Government	335	27.4	377	28.1	376	91.9	27.5	(0.5)	12.8
Central Bank	4	0.4	4	0.3	4	0.9	0.3	(2.1)	(17.8)
Corporate	29	2.4	30	2.2	30	7.2	2.2	(0.8)	1.1
Korea, Rep. of									
Total	2,253	150.3	2,315	152.8	2,347	100.0	156.4	2.6	5.7
Treasury and Other Government	859	57.3	892	58.9	904	38.5	60.2	2.5	6.7
Central Bank	97	6.5	94	6.2	94	4.0	6.3	1.8	(1.3)
Corporate	1,296	86.5	1,329	87.7	1,349	57.5	89.9	2.7	5.5
Malaysia									
Total	410	125.6	433	152.8	419	100.0	126.7	2.0	8.2
Treasury and Other Government	230	70.6	247	58.9	239	57.1	72.3	2.2	9.8
Central Bank	0.2	0.1	0.5	6.2	3	0.6	0.8	500.0	1,311.8
Corporate	179	54.9	186	87.7	177	42.3	53.6	0.7	4.7
Philippines									
Total	196	52.4	212	50.9	212	100.0	50.4	1.3	8.3
Treasury and Other Government	158	42.3	173	41.5	175	82.4	41.6	2.3	10.7
Central Bank	10	2.8	10	2.4	8	4.0	2.0	(15.8)	(17.4)
Corporate	28	7.4	29	6.9	29	13.6	6.6	1.2	4.1
Singapore									
Total	449	101.2	504	103.8	504	100.0	105.8	1.7	9.3
Treasury and Other Government	163	36.7	175	36.0	180	35.6	37.7	4.4	7.4
Central Bank	158	35.7	195	40.1	198	39.2	41.5	3.1	21.4
Corporate	128	28.8	134	27.6	127	25.2	26.6	(3.8)	(3.2)
Thailand									
Total	427	90.4	466	90.6	459	100.0	91.8	1.9	7.6
Treasury and Other Government	234	49.6	264	51.2	257	56.0	51.4	1.1	9.9
Central Bank	73	15.4	68	13.2	67	14.6	13.4	1.8	(7.6)
Corporate	120	25.4	135	26.2	135	29.3	26.9	3.6	12.3
Viet Nam									
Total	101	26.3	112	27.3	107	100.0	25.7	(4.5)	7.6
Treasury and Other Government	66	17.3	76	18.5	78	72.7	18.7	2.3	19.2
Central Bank	4	1.2	5	1.1	0	0.0	0.0	(100.0)	(100.0)
Corporate	30	7.9	31	7.6	29	27.3	7.0	(6.6)	(2.2)
Emerging East Asia									
Total	22,906	100.7	23,768	102.4	23,147	100.0	103.1	2.0	7.9
Treasury and Other Government	13,967	61.4	14,723	63.5	14,359	62.0	64.0	2.3	10.2
Central Bank	501	2.2	533	2.3	532	2.3	2.4	1.1	5.6
Corporate	8,438	37.1	8,512	36.7	8,256	35.7	36.8	1.4	4.3
Japan									
Total	9,669	237.2	10,184	240.5	9,358	100.0	236.9	(0.2)	2.9
Treasury and Other Government	8,923	218.9	9,409	222.2	8,654	92.5	219.0	(0.1)	3.1
Central Bank	43	1.1	33	0.8	14	0.1	0.3	(54.1)	(66.1)
Corporate	702	17.2	742	17.5	691	7.4	17.5	1.1	4.6

( ) = negative, – = not applicable, GDP = gross domestic product, q-o-q = quarter-on-quarter, Q1 = first quarter, Q2 = second quarter, USD = United States dollar, y-o-y = year-on-year.
Notes:
1. For Singapore, corporate bonds outstanding are based on *AsianBondsOnline* estimates.
2. Corporate bonds include issues by financial institutions.
3. Data for GDP is from CEIC Data Company.
4. Bloomberg LP end-of-period local currency–USD rates are used.
5. Growth rates are calculated from a local currency base and do not include currency effects. For emerging East Asia, growth figures are based on 30 June 2023 currency exchange rates and do not include currency effects.

Sources: People's Republic of China (CEIC Data Company); Hong Kong, China (Hong Kong Monetary Authority); Indonesia (Bank Indonesia; Directorate General of Budget Financing and Risk Management, Ministry of Finance; and Indonesia Stock Exchange); Republic of Korea (Bank of Korea and KG Zeroin Corporation); Malaysia (Bank Negara Malaysia); Philippines (Bureau of the Treasury and Bloomberg LP); Singapore (Monetary Authority of Singapore and Bloomberg LP); Thailand (Bank of Thailand); and Viet Nam (Bloomberg LP and Vietnam Bond Market Association).

decline in Indonesia's LCY bond market was largely driven by decreased government bond issuance as the government reduced its borrowing plan for 2023 on expected high revenue collection. Viet Nam's bond market witnessed a contraction of 4.5% q-o-q, primarily driven by a decline in corporate bonds as corporates remained wary of issuing bonds amid several regulatory changes. Growth in the region's corporate bond market eased to 1.4% q-o-q in Q2 2023 from 1.6% q-o-q in the previous quarter due to a sizeable amount of maturities in nearly all markets.

Total LCY bonds outstanding in Association of Southeast Asian Nations (ASEAN) markets reached USD2.1 trillion at the end of June, equivalent to 60.1% of ASEAN's annual aggregate output. ASEAN's share of the emerging East Asian LCY bond market declined slightly to 9.1% in Q2 2023 from 9.2% in Q1 2023 (**Figure 3**). The PRC remained home to the largest LCY bond market in emerging East Asia, with outstanding LCY bonds of USD18.3 trillion at the end of June, or the equivalent of 107.4% of the PRC's gross domestic product (GDP). The PRC's bond market also accounted for 79.2% of all emerging East Asian LCY bonds outstanding. Meanwhile, the Republic of Korea's LCY bond market, the region's second largest, reached a size of USD2.3 trillion (156.4% of GDP) at the end of June, comprising 10.1% of the regional total. In terms of the sectoral structure of the regional LCY bond market, Treasury and other government bonds totaled USD14.4 trillion at the end of June, accounting for 62.0% of all regional LCY bonds outstanding. Corporate

bonds comprised 35.7% of the region's total LCY bonds at the end of June, while central bank bonds accounted for the remaining 2.3% share.

Outstanding LCY Treasury bonds in emerging East Asia remained concentrated in medium- to long-term tenors. At the end of June, 53.2% of the region's Treasury bonds outstanding had maturities longer than 5 years (**Figure 4**). Treasury bonds outstanding in the region had a size-weighted average tenor of 8.5 years at the end of June, slightly higher than 8.3 years at the end of March. Except for the PRC and Hong Kong, China, all markets in the region had bond maturity profiles in which more than 50% of Treasury bonds outstanding carried tenors longer than 5 years. In the PRC and Hong Kong, China, Treasury bonds with maturities of 5 years or less comprised 52.9% and 84.4%, respectively, of total Treasury bonds outstanding.

Domestic investors expanded their holdings of emerging East Asian LCY Treasury bonds over the last year. Domestic investors collectively held 88.9% of regional LCY Treasury bonds at the end of June, up from 87.5% a year earlier. Over half of all LCY Treasury bonds in the region were held by banking institutions. By the end of June, the amount of LCY Treasury bonds

Figure 3: Local Currency Bonds Outstanding by Economy and Type of Bond as of 30 June 2023

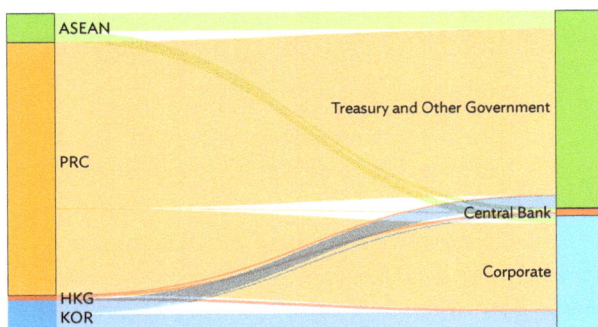

ASEAN = Association of Southeast Asian Nations; HKG = Hong Kong, China; KOR = Republic of Korea; PRC = People's Republic of China.
Note: ASEAN comprises the markets of Indonesia, Malaysia, the Philippines, Singapore, Thailand, and Viet Nam.
Source: *AsianBondsOnline* calculations based on various local sources.

Figure 4: Maturity Structure of Local Currency Treasury Bonds Outstanding in Select Emerging East Asian Markets as of 30 June 2023

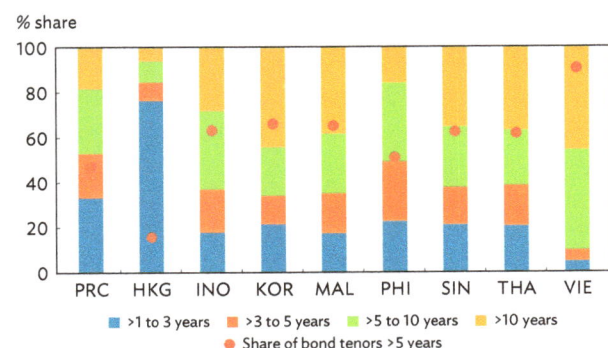

HKG = Hong Kong, China; INO = Indonesia; KOR = Republic of Korea; MAL = Malaysia; PHI = Philippines; PRC = People's Republic of China; SIN = Singapore; THA = Thailand; VIE = Viet Nam.
Note: Treasury bonds are local-currency-denominated fixed income securities with maturities longer than 1-year and issued by the national government.
Sources: People's Republic of China (Bloomberg LP); Hong Kong, China (Hong Kong Monetary Authority); Indonesia (Directorate General of Budget Financing and Risk Management, Ministry of Finance); Republic of Korea (Bloomberg LP); Malaysia (Bank Negara Malaysia Fully Automated System for Issuing/Tendering); Philippines (Bureau of the Treasury); Singapore (Monetary Authority of Singapore); Thailand (Bank of Thailand); and Viet Nam (Bloomberg LP).

Figure 5: Investor Profiles of Local Currency Treasury Bonds in Select Emerging East Asian Markets

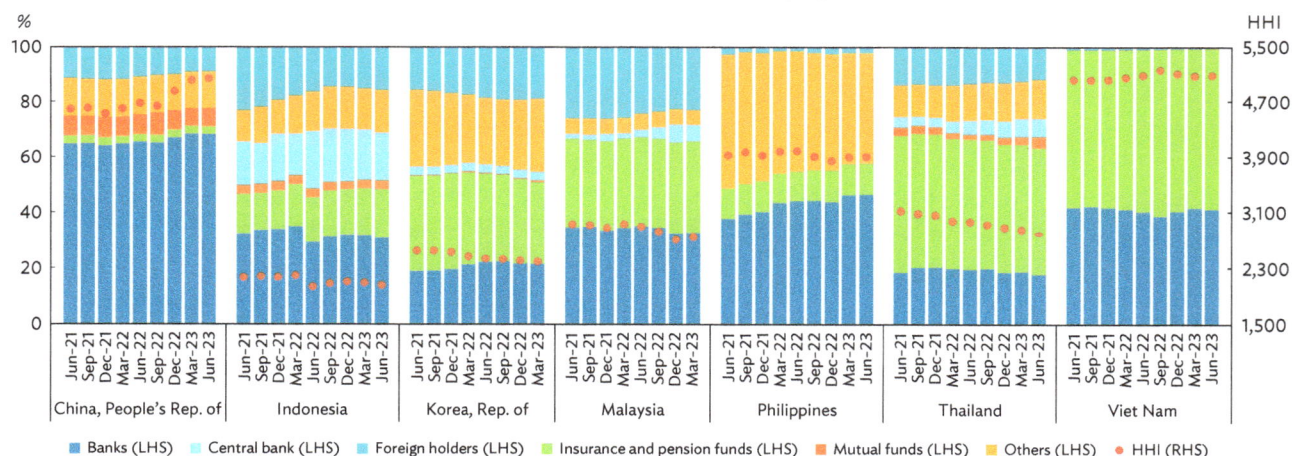

LHS = left-hand side, HHI = Herfindahl–Hirschman Index, RHS = right-hand side.
Notes:
1. Data for the Republic of Korea and Malaysia are up to March 2023.
2. "Others" include government institutions, individuals, securities companies, custodians, private corporations, and all other investors not elsewhere classified.
3. The Herfindahl–Hirschman Index is a commonly accepted measure of market concentration. In this case, the index was used to measure the investor profile diversification of the local currency bond markets and is calculated by summing the squared share of each investor group in the bond market.

Sources: People's Republic of China (CEIC Data Company); Indonesia (Directorate General of Budget Financing and Risk Management, Ministry of Finance); Republic of Korea (Bank of Korea); Malaysia (Bank Negara Malaysia); Philippines (Bureau of the Treasury); Thailand (Bank of Thailand); and Viet Nam (Ministry of Finance).

held by domestic banks was nearly 70% in the PRC; over 40% in the Philippines and Viet Nam; and around 31% in Indonesia, where the most diversified investor base was observed as measured by the Herfindahl–Hirschman Index of investor types (**Figure 5**). The next largest domestic investor group in the region comprised insurance firms and pension funds, which held a 12.1% share of regional LCY government bonds. The bond holdings share of insurance and pension funds was the largest in Viet Nam (58.1%); followed by Thailand (45.6%); Malaysia (33.1%); and the Republic of Korea (29.4%), where insurance and pension funds were the largest investor group, respectively. Moreover, lingering uncertainties over the US Federal Reserve's monetary tightening path resulted in a decline in the foreign holdings share in some regional markets in recent quarters. Overall, LCY bond markets in the region continue to develop with a more diversified investor base as reflected by the decline of the Herfindahl–Hirschman Index in many markets.

Section 2. Local Currency Bond Issuance

Emerging East Asia's LCY bond issuance reached USD2.4 trillion in Q2 2023 on moderated issuance growth. Overall growth of regional LCY bond issuance eased from 6.2% q-o-q and 12.2% y-o-y in Q1 2023 to

4.6% q-o-q and 3.5% y-o-y in Q2 2023. The region's aggregate LCY bond issuance in Q2 2023 was equivalent to 74.8% of total issuance in the US (USD3.1 trillion) and over two times that of the EU-20's aggregate LCY issuance (USD1.0 trillion). In ASEAN markets, LCY bond issuance contracted 6.5% q-o-q in Q2 2023, a reversal from the 7.7% q-o-q growth in Q1 2023. As a result, ASEAN's share of the region's LCY bond issuance fell to 20.0% in Q2 2023 from 22.4% in Q1 2023 (**Figure 6**).

The region's LCY government bond issuance totaled USD980.0 billion in Q2 2023 on marginal growth of 2.2% q-o-q, following a 12.4% q-o-q increase in Q1 2023 (**Figure 7**). While the PRC accounted for 85.4% of regional total government bond issuance, supported by increases in Treasury and local government bond issuance, the growth eased to 2.7% q-o-q in Q2 2023 from 10.8% q-o-q in Q1 2023 on reduced issuance of policy bank bonds. Government bond issuance in ASEAN markets (USD87.3 billion) shrank 12.5% q-o-q in Q2 2023, and their share in total regional government bonds fell to 8.9% in Q2 2023 from 10.4% in the previous quarter. Four out of six ASEAN markets saw reduced government bond issuance in Q2 2023, as governments frontloaded their financing needs in Q1 2023. Meanwhile, the Republic of Korea posted a 27.2% q-o-q increase in government bond issuance

Figure 6: Local Currency Bond Issuance in Select Emerging East Asian Markets

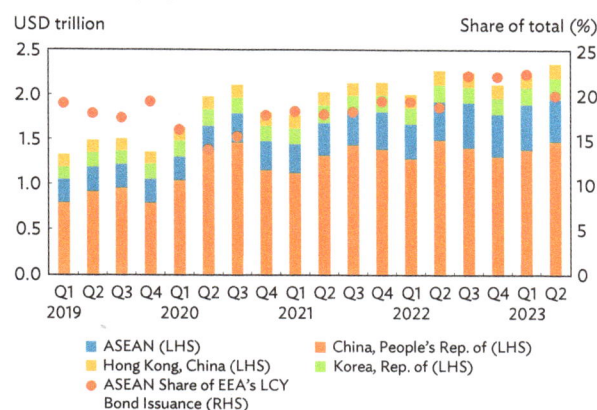

ASEAN = Association of Southeast Asian Nations, EEA = emerging East Asia, LCY = local currency, LHS = left-hand side, Q1 = first quarter, Q2 = second quarter, Q3 = third quarter, Q4 = fourth quarter, RHS = right-hand side, USD = United States dollar.

Notes:
1. ASEAN comprises the markets of Indonesia, Malaysia, the Philippines, Singapore, Thailand, and Viet Nam.
2. Figures were computed based on 30 June 2023 currency exchange rates and do not include currency effects.

Source: People's Republic of China (CEIC); Hong Kong, China (Hong Kong Monetary Authority); Indonesia (Bank Indonesia, Directorate General of Budget Financing and Risk Management, Ministry of Finance; and Indonesia Stock Exchange); Republic of Korea (Bank of Korea and KG Zeroin Corporation); Malaysia (Bank Negara Malaysia); Philippines (Bureau of the Treasury and Bloomberg LP); Singapore (Monetary Authority of Singapore and Bloomberg LP); Thailand (Bank of Thailand and ThaiBMA); and Viet Nam (Vietnam Bond Market Association and Bloomberg LP).

Figure 7: Local Currency Bond Issuance by Economy and Type of Bond in the Second Quarter of 2023

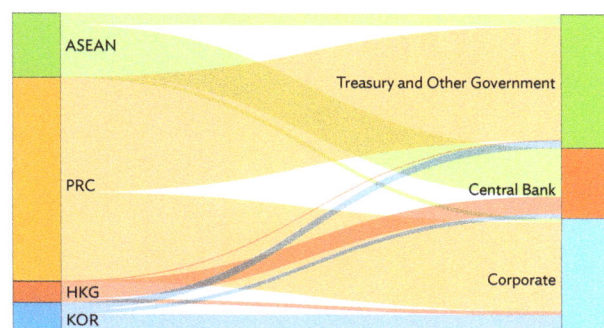

ASEAN = Association of Southeast Asian Nations; HKG = Hong Kong, China; KOR = Republic of Korea; PRC = People's Republic of China.

Note: ASEAN comprises the markets of Indonesia, Malaysia, the Philippines, Singapore, Thailand, and Viet Nam.

Source: *AsianBondsOnline* calculations based on various local sources.

in Q2 2023, as the government aimed to utilize 65% of its budget expenditures in the first half of the year. Central bank bond issuance in the region comprised 21.7% of the region's total LCY issuance in Q2 2023. ASEAN economies accounted for a 69.2% share of total central bank bond issuance in the region, led by the Monetary Authority of Singapore. The Hong Kong Monetary Authority was the second-largest central bank bond issuer in the region, accounting for 24.9% of emerging East Asia's central bank issuance during the quarter.

LCY corporate bond issuance in the region rebounded in Q2 2023 due to refinancing needs. Total corporate bond issuance in emerging East Asia reached USD861.2 billion in Q2 2023, rising 12.6% q-o-q, a reversal from the 1.1% q-o-q contraction in Q1 2023 (**Table 2**). Most regional markets posted higher issuance volumes in Q2 2023 amid large corporate bond maturities, which resulted in slower corporate bond outstanding growth. The PRC continued to be the largest corporate bond issuer in the region with a share of 75.6%. Corporate bond issuance in the PRC rose 11.8% q-o-q in Q2 2023, following a 0.6% q-o-q decline in Q1 2023. The Republic of Korea, with a share of 17.7% of the regional total, also posted accelerated growth of 28.0% q-o-q in Q2 2023 from a 6.2% q-o-q contraction in the previous quarter. ASEAN economies registered growth in corporate bond issuance of 9.1% q-o-q, reversing a contraction of 23.3% q-o-q in Q1 2023.

Treasury bond issuance in emerging East Asia in Q2 2023 remained concentrated in medium- to long-term financing. In Q2 2023, 54.8% of Treasury bond issuance in the region had tenors of more than 5 years (**Figure 8**). Treasury bonds issued in the region during the quarter had a size-weighted average maturity of 6.7 years, similar to the average of 6.9 years in Q1 2023. In Viet Nam, tenors of 5 years and above accounted for 96.1% of Treasury bond issuance (**Figure 9**).

Section 3. Intra-Regional Bond Issuance

Intra-regional bond issuance in emerging East Asia increased to USD13.0 billion in Q2 2023 from USD11.1 billion in Q1 2023 (Figure 10).[4] Total intra-regional bond issuance in Q2 2023 was double the USD6.5 billion of issuance in Q2 2022. Monthly intra-regional issuance reached USD4.4 billion in April and

---

[4] Intra-regional bond issuance is defined as emerging East Asian bond issuance denominated in a member's currency excluding the issuer's home currency.

Table 2: Local-Currency-Denominated Bond Issuance (gross)

	Q2 2022		Q1 2023		Q2 2023		Growth Rate (%)	
							Q2 2023	
	Amount (USD billion)	% share	Amount (USD billion)	% share	Amount (USD billion)	% share	q-o-q	y-o-y
China, People's Rep. of								
Total	1,629	100.0	1,475	100.0	1,488	100.0	6.5	(1.1)
Treasury and Other Government	996	61.1	860	58.3	837	56.2	2.7	(9.0)
Central Bank	0	0.0	0	0.0	0	0.0	–	–
Corporate	633	38.9	615	41.7	651	43.8	11.8	11.4
Hong Kong, China								
Total	156	100.0	161	100.0	156	100.0	(3.2)	(0.5)
Treasury and Other Government	4	2.3	1	0.6	1	0.8	21.8	(66.7)
Government	121	77.3	124	77.3	127	81.7	2.2	5.1
Corporate	32	20.4	35	22.0	27	17.6	(22.9)	(14.2)
Indonesia								
Total	34	100.0	36	100.0	23	100.0	(35.7)	(31.5)
Treasury and Other Government	10	29.1	16	45.1	10	43.4	(38.1)	2.4
Central Bank	22	65.0	18	49.8	12	52.0	(33.0)	(45.2)
Corporate	2	6.0	2	5.0	1	4.6	(41.3)	(47.1)
Korea, Rep. of								
Total	191	100.0	190	100.0	237	100.0	26.6	26.1
Treasury and Other Government	61	31.9	44	23.0	55	23.2	27.2	(8.5)
Central Bank	18	9.6	26	13.5	30	12.7	18.6	67.2
Corporate	112	58.5	120	63.4	152	64.2	28.0	38.4
Malaysia								
Total	25	100.0	23	100.0	25	100.0	12.1	3.9
Treasury and Other Government	15	59.8	16	68.0	13	53.6	(11.6)	(6.9)
Central Bank	0.2	0.8	0.5	2.0	3	10.5	500.0	1,311.8
Corporate	10	39.4	7	30.0	9	35.9	33.9	(5.4)
Philippines								
Total	44	100.0	50	100.0	39	100.0	(19.2)	(9.2)
Treasury and Other Government	10	23.6	17	34.8	10	26.3	(39.0)	1.3
Central Bank	32	72.6	32	64.3	28	70.7	(11.2)	(11.6)
Corporate	2	3.8	0.4	0.9	1	3.0	177.6	(29.1)
Singapore								
Total	243	100.0	295	100.0	310	100.0	6.9	24.5
Treasury and Other Government	30	12.2	29	9.9	34	10.8	16.7	10.4
Central Bank	209	86.2	264	89.4	276	88.8	6.2	28.2
Corporate	4	1.5	2	0.7	1	0.4	(43.9)	(69.4)
Thailand								
Total	61	100.0	68	100.0	70	100.0	7.1	14.3
Treasury and Other Government	20	32.0	18	26.3	18	25.5	4.1	(8.7)
Central Bank	25	40.5	34	50.1	35	49.8	6.4	40.6
Corporate	17	27.6	16	23.6	17	24.7	12.0	2.4
Viet Nam								
Total	12	100.0	40	100.0	3	100.0	(93.4)	(76.7)
Treasury and Other Government	1	12.1	6	13.8	2	78.6	(62.0)	50.9
Central Bank	7	62.1	34	83.2	0	0.0	(100.0)	(100.0)
Corporate	3	25.8	1	3.0	0.6	21.4	(52.9)	(80.7)
Emerging East Asia								
Total	2,395	100.0	2,338	100.0	2,352	100.0	4.6	3.5
Treasury and Other Government	1,146	47.9	1,006	43.1	980	41.7	2.2	(8.3)
Central Bank	435	18.1	532	22.7	510	21.7	(2.9)	16.0
Corporate	814	34.0	799	34.2	861	36.6	12.6	12.8
Japan								
Total	412	100.0	489	100.0	380	100.0	(15.7)	(2.0)
Treasury and Other Government	368	89.3	466	95.2	349	91.9	(18.6)	0.8
Central Bank	16	3.9	0	0.0	0	0.0	–	(100.0)
Corporate	28	6.7	23	4.8	31	8.1	43.5	17.7

( ) = negative, – = not applicable, Q1 = first quarter, Q2 = second quarter, q-o-q = quarter-on-quarter, USD = United States dollar, y-o-y = year-on-year.
Notes:
1. Corporate bonds include issues by financial institutions.
2. Bloomberg LP end-of-period local currency–USD rates are used.
3. Growth rates are calculated from local currency base and do not include currency effects. For emerging East Asia, growth figures are based on 30 June 2023 currency exchange rates and do not include currency effects.

Source: People's Republic of China (CEIC Data Company); Hong Kong, China (Hong Kong Monetary Authority); Indonesia (Bank Indonesia, Directorate General of Budget Financing and Risk Management, Ministry of Finance; and Indonesia Stock Exchange); Republic of Korea (Bank of Korea and KG Zeroin Corporation); Malaysia (Bank Negara Malaysia); Philippines (Bureau of the Treasury and Bloomberg LP); Singapore (Monetary Authority of Singapore and Bloomberg LP); Thailand (Bank of Thailand and ThaiBMA); Viet Nam (Vietnam Bond Market Association and Bloomberg LP); and Japan (Japan Securities Dealers Association).

Figure 8: Maturity Structure of Local Currency Treasury Bond Issuance in Emerging East Asia

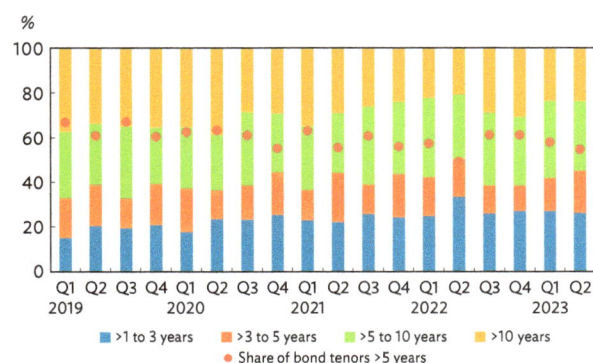

Q1 = first quarter, Q2 = second quarter, Q3 = third quarter, Q4 = fourth quarter.

Notes:

1. Figures were computed based on 30 June 2023 currency exchange rates and do not include currency effects.
2. Treasury bonds are local-currency-denominated fixed-income securities with maturities longer than 1 year and issued by the national government.

Source: *AsianBondsOnline* calculations based on various local sources.

Figure 10: Intra-Regional Bond Issuance in Select Emerging East Asian Economies

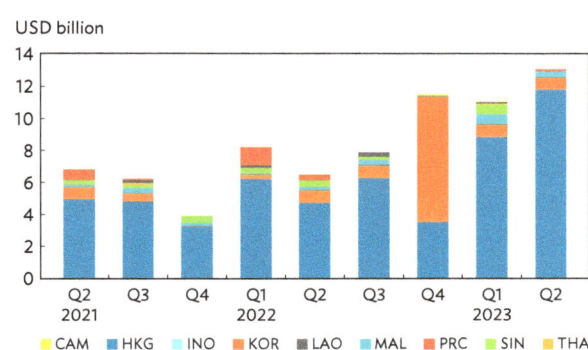

CAM = Cambodia; HKG = Hong Kong, China; INO = Indonesia; KOR = Republic of Korea; LAO = Lao People's Democratic Republic; MAL = Malaysia; PRC = People's Republic of China; Q1 = first quarter; Q2 = second quarter; Q3 = third quarter; Q4 = fourth quarter; SIN = Singapore; THA = Thailand; USD = United States dollar.

Source: *AsianBondsOnline* calculations based on Bloomberg LP data.

Figure 9: Maturity Structure of Local Currency Treasury Bond Issuance in Emerging East Asia by Market in the Second Quarter of 2023

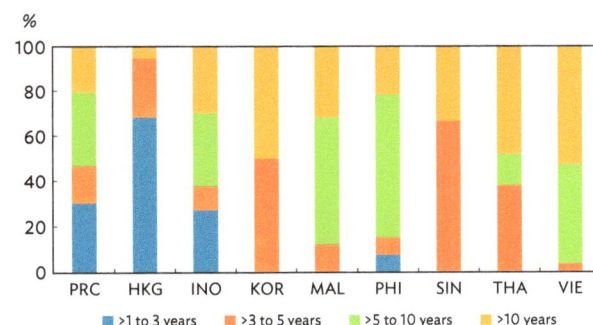

HKG = Hong Kong, China; INO = Indonesia; KOR = Republic of Korea; MAL = Malaysia; PHI = Philippines; PRC = People's Republic of China; SIN = Singapore; THA = Thailand; VIE = Viet Nam.

Note: Treasury bonds are local currency-denominated fixed income securities with maturities longer than 1-year and issued by the national government.

Source: *AsianBondsOnline* calculations based on various local sources.

Figure 11: Intra-Regional Bond Issuance in Emerging East Asia by Economy, Currency, and Sector in the Second Quarter of 2023

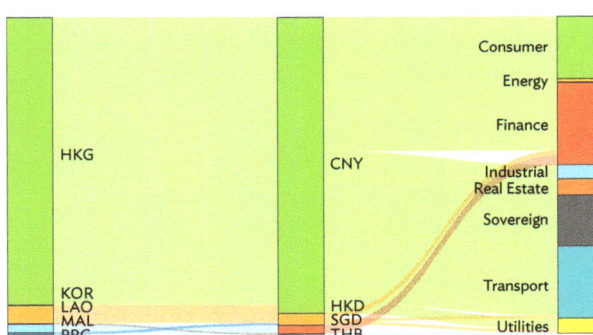

CNY = Chinese yuan; HKD = Hong Kong dollar; HKG = Hong Kong, China; KOR = Republic of Korea; LAO = Lao People's Democratic Republic; MAL = Malaysia; PRC = People's Republic of China; SGD = Singapore dollar; THB = Thai baht.

Source: *AsianBondsOnline* calculations based on Bloomberg LP data.

USD4.3 billion in both May and June. Increased intra-regional bond issuance in Q2 2023 was mainly driven by Hong Kong, China, whose bond issuance rose 33.1% q-o-q, offsetting decreased issuance in the Republic of Korea, Malaysia, and the Lao People's Democratic Republic. The PRC resumed intra-regional bond issuance during the quarter with USD0.1 billion of issuance via a single-tranche bond from CMB International. Hong Kong, China was the region's largest issuer of intra-regional bonds during the quarter with a total issuance volume of

USD11.8 billion, accounting for 90.5% of the regional total. China Merchants Group, a state-owned logistics company domiciled in Hong Kong, China, was the largest issuer of intra-regional bonds during the quarter with aggregate issuance of USD2.8 billion.

The Chinese yuan remained the region's dominant currency for intra-regional bond issuance in Q2 2023. CNY-denominated issuance totaled USD12.2 billion, coming entirely from Hong Kong, China and the Republic of Korea, and accounting for 93.3% of the regional total (**Figure 11**). Other intra-regional issuances were denominated in Hong Kong dollars, Singapore dollars, and Thai baht, which collectively accounted for 6.7% of the total intra-regional issuance in emerging East Asia.

In Q2 2023, issuance of intra-regional bonds in emerging East Asia was mostly distributed in four sectors. The financial sector remained the largest source of intra-regional bonds in the region despite a contraction of 15.9% q-o-q in Q2 2023 on issuance of USD3.4 billion (26.1% regional share) versus USD4.0 billion in Q1 2023. The transportation sector was the second-largest issuer of intra-regional bonds with USD3.0 billion (22.9% regional share), which was down from USD3.4 billion in the prior quarter. The consumer sector and sovereign issuers were the third- and fourth-largest sources of intra-regional bonds in Q2 2023, respectively, accounting for 19.9% and 15.9% of the regional total.

Section 4. G3 Currency Bond Issuance

Issuance of G3 currency bonds in emerging East Asia totaled USD36.9 billion in Q2 2023, 36.9% lower than the USD58.4 billion issued in Q1 2023 (Figure 12). USD-denominated issuance accounted for 81.7% of

the region's G3 currency bond issuance in Q2 2023, despite contracting 55.1% y-o-y. Compared with Q2 2022, total G3 currency bond issuance contracted 49.7% due to high interest rates. The PRC witnessed a 72.9% y-o-y contraction in its G3 currency issuance. The Republic of Korea surpassed the PRC and became the region's largest G3 currency bond issuer during the quarter. ASEAN markets' G3 currency bond issuance fell 52.2% y-o-y to USD7.2 billion in Q2 2023, accounting for 19.5% of the regional total (**Figure 13**). Among ASEAN markets, Malaysia and Indonesia had the highest issuance of G3 currency bonds at USD3.4 billion and USD2.1 billion, respectively. Cambodia, the Lao People's Democratic Republic, the Philippines, and Viet Nam had no issuance of G3 currency bonds during the review period.

Figure 13: G3 Currency Bond Issuance in Emerging East Asia in the Second Quarter of 2023

KOR 35.5%
MAL 9.2%
ASEAN 19.5%
INO 5.6%
THA 1.1%
PRC 31.6%
SIN 3.6%
HKG 13.4%

ASEAN = Association of Southeast Asian Nations; HKG = Hong Kong, China; INO = Indonesia; KOR = Republic of Korea; MAL = Malaysia; PRC = People's Republic of China; SIN = Singapore; THA = Thailand.
Note: G3 currency bonds are denominated in either euros, Japanese yen, or United States dollars.
Source: *AsianBondsOnline* calculations based on Bloomberg LP data.

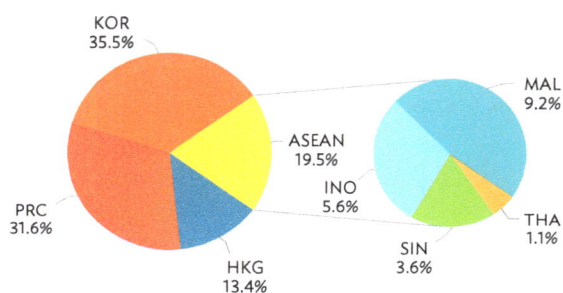

Figure 12: Monthly G3 Currency Bond Issuance in Select Emerging East Asian Markets

USD billion

EUR = euro, JPY = Japanese yen, USD = United States dollar.
Notes:
1. Emerging East Asia comprises Cambodia; the People's Republic of China; Hong Kong, China; Indonesia; the Republic of Korea; the Lao People's Democratic Republic; Malaysia; the Philippines; Singapore; Thailand; and Viet Nam.
2. G3 currency bonds are denominated in either euros, Japanese yen, or United States dollars.
3. Figures were computed based on 30 June 2023 currency exchange rates and do not include currency effects.
Source: *AsianBondsOnline* calculations based on Bloomberg LP data.

Section 5. Yield Curve Movements

Between 1 June and 31 August, LCY government bond yield curves shifted upward in most regional markets (Figure 14). During the review period, continued monetary tightening, elevated inflation, and resilient economic indicators in the US pushed up regional yields. The exceptions to the regional trend were the PRC and Viet Nam. Both the PRC's and Viet Nam's yields fell following key interest rate reductions by their respective central banks in June and additional interest rate cuts in August for the PRC.

Figure 14: Benchmark Yield Curves—Local Currency Government Bonds

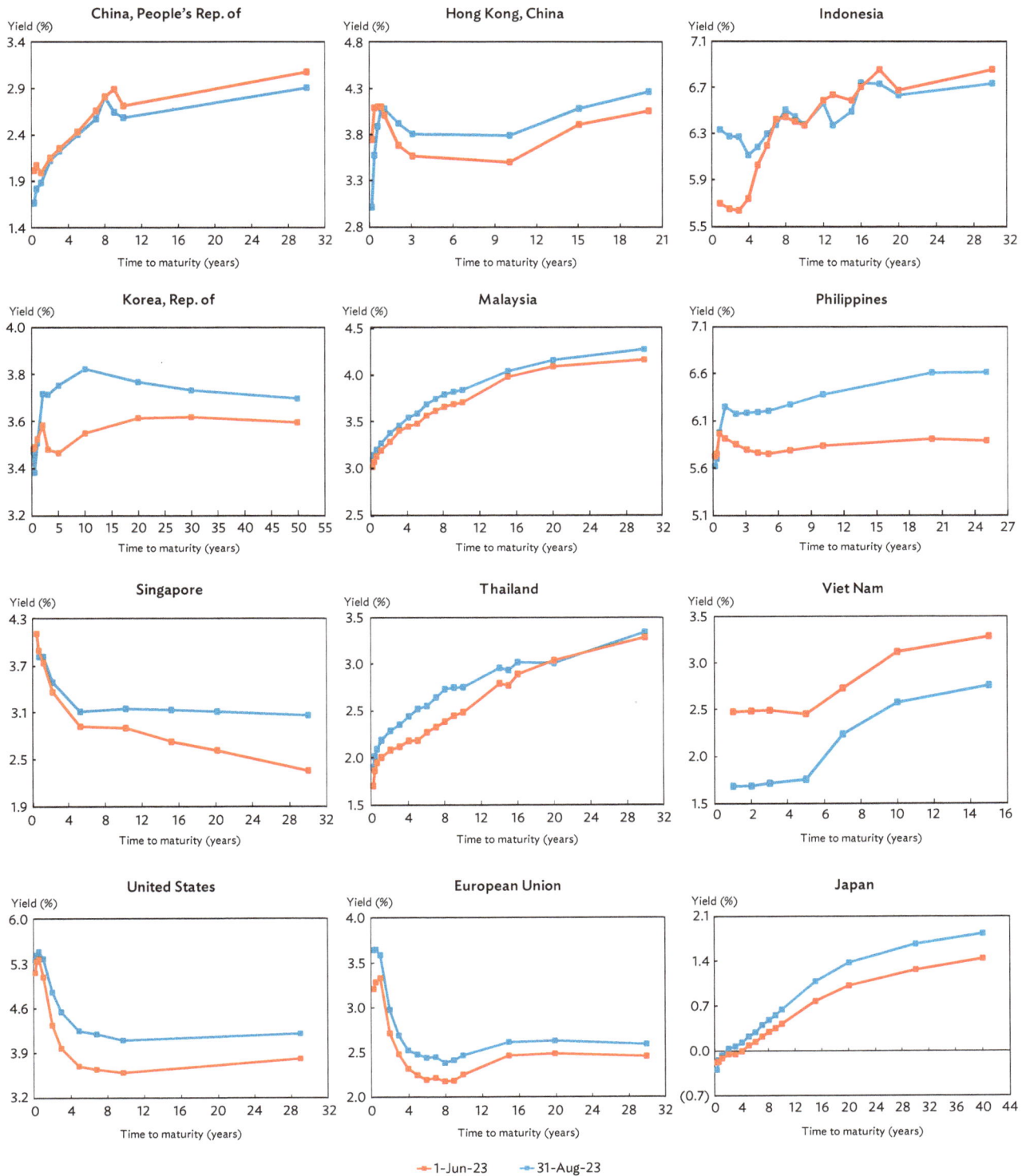

China, People's Rep. of

Hong Kong, China

Indonesia

Korea, Rep. of

Malaysia

Philippines

Singapore

Thailand

Viet Nam

United States

European Union

Japan

● 1-Jun-23   ● 31-Aug-23

( ) = negative.
Sources: Based on data from Bloomberg LP and Thai Bond Market Association.

Recent Developments in ASEAN+3 Sustainable Bond Markets

Sustainable bonds outstanding in ASEAN+3 markets reached USD694.4 billion at the end of June 2023.[5] Growth of 31.5% year-on-year and 5.1% quarter-on-quarter (q-o-q) were recorded in the second quarter (Q2) of 2023. The q-o-q expansion was roughly in line with the growth in the global sustainable bond market of 5.5% q-o-q during the same period, bringing total global sustainable bonds outstanding to USD3.6 trillion at the end of June. The ASEAN+3 sustainable bond market maintained its 19.1% share of the global total at the end of June. However, ASEAN+3's growth in Q2 2023 was slower compared to the world's largest regional sustainable bond market, the European Union 20 (EU-20), which expanded 7.2% q-o-q to reach USD1.4 trillion at the end of June. The EU-20 comprised a 38.5% share of the global sustainable bond market at the end of the

review period (**Figure 15**). Despite its rapid growth, the ASEAN+3 sustainable bond market accounted for only 1.9% of total ASEAN+3 bonds outstanding at the end of June, which was also much lower than the corresponding share of 6.6% in EU-20 markets.

The ASEAN+3 sustainable bond market has potential for further development to provide more local currency (LCY) and long-term financing. At the end of June, green bonds (64.3%), LCY financing (65.1%), and short-term (maturity of less than 5 years) financing (75.6%) comprised a majority of ASEAN+3 sustainable bonds outstanding (**Figure 16**). The EU-20's sustainable bond market was roughly similar with respect to green bonds (63.2%), but it had a higher share of LCY financing (89.8%) and long-term (maturity of more than 5 years) financing (59.6%) (**Figure 17**). ASEAN+3's outstanding

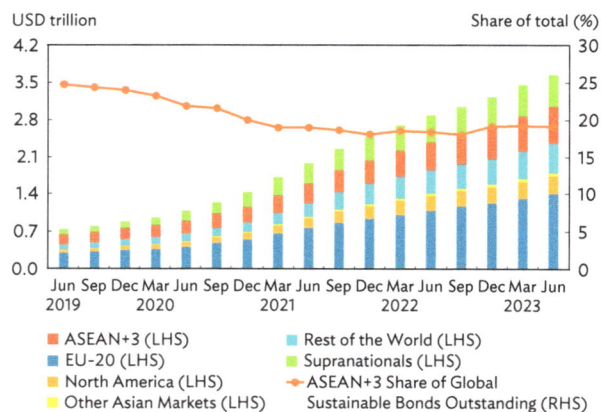

Figure 15: Global Sustainable Bonds Outstanding

ASEAN+3 = Association of Southeast Asian Nations plus the People's Republic of China; Hong Kong, China; Japan; and the Republic of Korea; EU = European Union; LHS = left-hand side; RHS = right-hand side; USD = United States dollar.
Notes:
1. EU-20 includes EU member markets Austria, Belgium, Croatia, Cyprus, Estonia, Finland, France, Germany, Greece, Ireland, Italy, Latvia, Lithuania, Luxembourg, Malta, the Netherlands, Portugal, Slovakia, Slovenia, and Spain.
2. Data include both local currency and foreign currency issues.
Source: *AsianBondsOnline* calculations based on Bloomberg LP data.

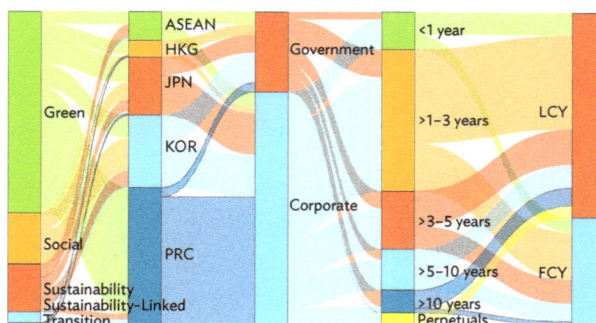

Figure 16: Market Profile of Outstanding ASEAN+3 Sustainable Bonds at the End of June 2023

ASEAN = Association of Southeast Asian Nations; FCY = foreign currency; HKG = Hong Kong, China; JPN = Japan; KOR = Republic of Korea; LCY = local currency; PRC = People's Republic of China.
Notes:
1. ASEAN+3 is defined to include member states of the Association of Southeast Asian Nations (ASEAN) plus the People's Republic of China; Hong Kong, China; Japan; and the Republic of Korea.
2. ASEAN comprises the markets of Indonesia, the Lao People's Democratic Republic, Malaysia, the Philippines, Singapore, Thailand, and Viet Nam.
Source: *AsianBondsOnline* calculations based on Bloomberg LP data.

---

[5] ASEAN+3 is defined to include member states of the Association of Southeast Asian Nations (ASEAN) plus the People's Republic of China; Hong Kong, China; Japan; and the Republic of Korea.

sustainable bonds had a weighted-average tenor of 4.4 years at the end of June versus 8.6 years for the EU-20.

ASEAN+3 sustainable bond issuance rebounded in Q2 2023, buoyed by a surge in the issuance of social bonds. Sustainable bond issuance in the region tallied USD69.0 billion in Q2 2023, with growth accelerating to 19.7% q-o-q following a 0.6% q-o-q contraction in the first quarter of 2022. This led to an uptick in ASEAN+3's share of global sustainable bond issuance to 26.8% in Q2 2023 from 23.0% in the prior quarter (**Figure 18**). Social bonds witnessed growth of 86.6% q-o-q in Q2 2023 on total issuance of USD16.5 billion, driven largely by issuances from the Republic of Korea and Japan. The People's Republic of China's sustainable bond market remained the largest in the region in terms of issuance, accounting for 44.3% of the regional total during Q2 2023. ASEAN markets' sustainable bond issuance contracted 53.4% q-o-q in Q2 2023, with their collective share slipping to only 4.6% of the regional issuance total. This, however, was higher than their 2.0% share of the region's general bond issuance.

ASEAN+3 sustainable bond issuance in Q2 2023 was mostly LCY-denominated (Figure 19). LCY issuance comprised 78.4% of ASEAN+3 sustainable bond issuance during the quarter. This, however, was lower

than the 97.2% LCY share of issuance in the general bond market and the 86.6% share in the EU-20 sustainable bond market during the same period. Markets in the People's Republic of China and Japan had over 90% of sustainable bonds issued in Q2 2023 denominated in their respective domestic currencies. LCY sustainable bond issuance from ASEAN markets comprised 61.9% of their total issuance, compared with an 81.5% LCY share in

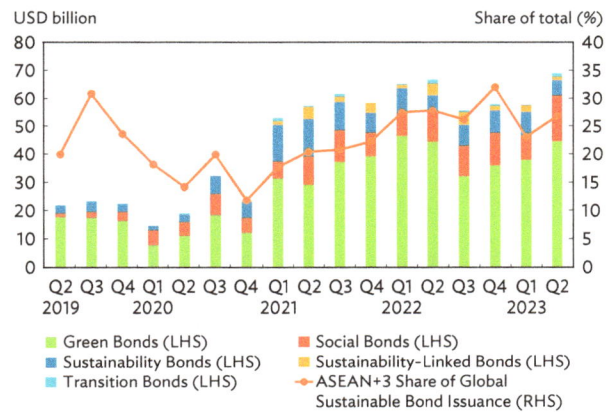

Figure 18: ASEAN+3 Sustainable Bond Issuance and Share of the Global Total

ASEAN+3 = Association of Southeast Asian Nations plus the People's Republic of China; Hong Kong, China; Japan; and the Republic of Korea; LHS = left-hand side; Q1 = first quarter; Q2 = second quarter; Q3 = third quarter; Q4 = fourth quarter; RHS = right-hand side; USD = United States dollar.
Note: Data include both local currency and foreign currency issues.
Source: *AsianBondsOnline* calculations based on Bloomberg LP data.

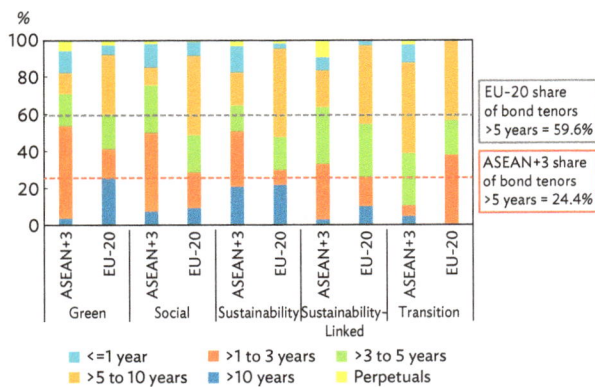

Figure 17: Maturity Profile of ASEAN+3 and EU-20 Sustainable Bonds Outstanding at the End of June 2023

ASEAN+3 = Association of Southeast Asian Nations plus the People's Republic of China; Hong Kong, China; Japan; and the Republic of Korea; EU = European Union.
Notes:
1. EU-20 includes EU member markets Austria, Belgium, Croatia, Cyprus, Estonia, Finland, France, Germany, Greece, Ireland, Italy, Latvia, Lithuania, Luxembourg, Malta, the Netherlands, Portugal, Slovakia, Slovenia, and Spain.
2. Data include both local currency and foreign currency issues.
Source: *AsianBondsOnline* calculations based on Bloomberg LP data.

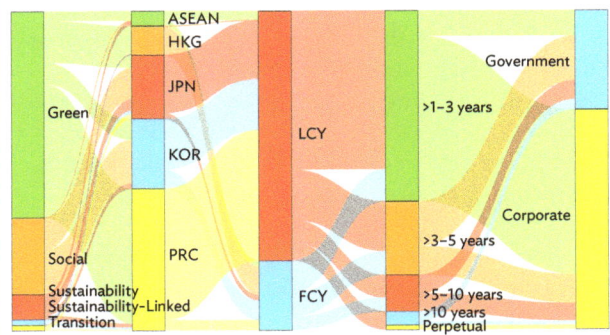

Figure 19: Market Profile of ASEAN+3 Sustainable Bond Issuance in the Second Quarter of 2023

ASEAN = Association of Southeast Asian Nations; FCY = foreign currency; HKG = Hong Kong, China; JPN = Japan; KOR = Republic of Korea; LCY = local currency; PRC = People's Republic of China.
Notes:
1. ASEAN+3 is defined to include member states of ASEAN plus the People's Republic of China; Hong Kong, China; Japan; and the Republic of Korea.
2. ASEAN comprises the markets of Indonesia, Malaysia, the Philippines, Singapore, Thailand, and Viet Nam.
Source: *AsianBondsOnline* calculations based on Bloomberg LP data.

general ASEAN bond markets. About 64% of ASEAN+3 sustainable LCY bond issuance had maturities of 3 years or less, which was higher than the corresponding share of foreign-currency-denominated sustainable bond issuance (46.2%). This reflects the need to develop the region's sustainable bond market to mobilize more long-term LCY financing. One way to further promote sustainable financing is through the use of blended finance. **Box 2** discusses the four types of blended financing and how this can help fund sustainable projects.

ASEAN+3 sustainable bond issuers focused mainly on seeking shorter-term financing in Q2 2023. More than 80% of the sustainable bonds issued in ASEAN+3 markets carried maturities of 5 years or less, reflecting the challenges in enticing long-term sustainable investment in the region. In contrast, the share of sustainable bond issuance with tenors of 5 years or less was only 27.7% in EU-20 markets in Q2 2023. The weighted-average tenor of ASEAN+3 sustainable bond issuance in Q2 2023 was 4.8 years compared with the EU-20's 9.1 years.

The private sector continued to dominate ASEAN+3 sustainable bond issuance in Q2 2023. The share of private sector issuance in total regional sustainable bond issuance was 69.0% in Q2 2023. This was much higher than the private sector's share of 29.2% for ASEAN+3 general bond issuance in Q2 2023, signaling the public sector's potential to play a bigger role in the region's sustainable bond market.

Box 2: Promoting Innovative Climate Finance for Emerging and Developing Economies

It is increasingly clear that the Paris Agreement's long-term goals—which were negotiated by 196 parties at the United Nations Climate Change Conference in 2015—are becoming difficult to achieve without more ambitious global policy actions.[a] One of the key goals is to reduce greenhouse gas (GHG) emissions enough to keep the increase in the global average temperature this century to well below 2°C (compared with pre-industrial times), while striving to approach a gain of only 1.5°C. In line with this, many countries around the world have committed to net zero emissions or carbon neutrality by 2050 (or soon after).

Since 2021, the global economy has faced serious energy shortages amid the recovery from the coronavirus disease (COVID-19) pandemic. These shortages were subsequently exacerbated by the Russian invasion of Ukraine in February 2022. As a result, many countries have increased their dependence on carbon-intensive coals and other fossil fuels. Meanwhile, energy shortages have also hampered measures to address extreme poverty and inequality in low-income countries.

The substantially high cost of fossil fuels has reminded the world that investments in the clean and low-emission energy projects needed to achieve net zero GHG emissions have been inadequate for many years because of the limited scale of climate policies globally. While an increase in overdependence on fossil fuels might be inevitable for some time, the world is increasingly aware that accelerating the transition toward carbon neutrality is an urgent task.

More Financing is Needed for Emerging and Developing Economies

In general, emerging and developing economies (EMDEs) suffer from a lack of social and economic infrastructure. At present, energy consumption in EMDEs, excluding the People's Republic of China and India, is relatively low. However, energy demand is expected to grow significantly as industrialization, urbanization, and economic development continue to progress. EMDEs are set to account for the bulk of GHG emissions growth in the coming decades unless much stronger action is taken to transform their energy systems. In a scenario reflecting today's announced and existing climate and energy policies, GHG emissions from EMDEs are projected to grow by 5 gigatonnes over the next 2 decades, while they are projected to fall by 2 gigatonnes in developed countries and to plateau in the People's Republic of China during the same period (International Energy Agency 2021). Therefore, a massive increase in clean energy investment is required to put these countries on a pathway to net zero emissions in a cost-effective way.

Energy investments in EMDEs currently depend heavily on public sources of finance. At the 15th United Nations Framework Convention on Climate Change (COP15) held in 2009, developed countries committed to a collective goal of mobilizing USD100 billion per year by 2020 for climate action in EMDEs. This financial goal was formalized at the subsequent COP16 held in 2010. At COP21 held in 2015 in

---

[a] This box was written by Sayuri Shirai, a visiting fellow and advisor for sustainable policies at the Asian Development Bank Institute, a professor at the Faculty of Policy Management at Keio University, and a former policy board member of the Bank of Japan.

continued on next page

Box 2 *continued*

Paris, it was agreed to continue with the same USD100 billion amount annually until 2025. In 2020, however, the total amount of climate finance for EMDEs rose a mere 4% to USD83 billion; thus, the promised financial support has not yet materialized (**Figure B2.1**). Of this USD83 billion, public climate finance (both bilateral and multilateral) continued to take a substantial share of the total and accounted for 82% (Organisation for Economic Co-operation and Development 2022). Private climate finance mobilized for EMDEs decreased slightly to USD13 billion in 2020 and has remained lower than anticipated. To generate more climate finance for EMDEs, private funds need to be mobilized to a greater extent.

Figure B2.1: Total Climate Finance Provided and Mobilized

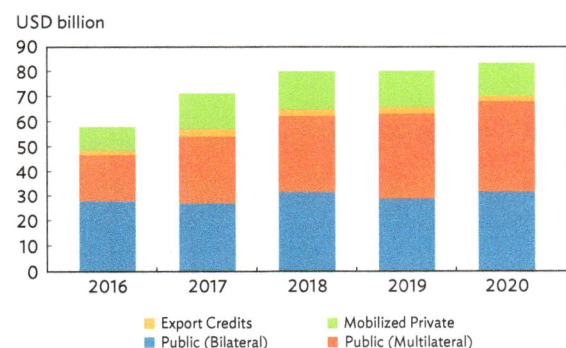

USD billion

Legend: Export Credits; Mobilized Private; Public (Bilateral); Public (Multilateral)

USD = United States dollar.
Source: Organisation for Economic Co-operation and Development.

Using Blended Finance to Mobilize Private Capital

Given this background, blended finance is under the spotlight again because of its potential to effectively utilize public and private capital jointly and deepen investors' involvement in global environmental and social projects. In recent years, momentum has been gathering in the world of private capital largely due to the rapid growth of institutional investors' environmental, social, and corporate governance (ESG) investments. ESG investors mainly comprise long-term asset owners (e.g., pension funds and insurance companies) and their asset management companies. In 2021, global-financial-sector-specific alliances—comprising asset owners, asset managers, banks, insurers, financial service providers, and investment consultants—formed the Glasgow Financial Alliance for Net Zero (GFANZ) as part of efforts to attain net zero GHG emissions from their financed activities by 2050. This initiative is contributing to the momentum of ESG investments that seek to encourage corporate behavioral and

business model changes. The focus of GFANZ members is gradually expanding beyond listed companies in developed countries, given that the global climate goals cannot be achieved without successful GHG reductions in EMDEs as well.

Since the global financial crisis, financial regulations have been tightened in many economies, making it more difficult for investors to take certain risks, including investment in EMDEs. The recent financial market turbulence as a result of rapid normalization of the massive monetary easing adopted during the COVID-19 pandemic has also reduced investor appetites. If the current situation is left unaddressed, it will delay EMDEs' responses to climate change and other environmental problems, hindering achievement of the sustainable development goals. In light of this, the United Nations convened the Net-Zero Asset Owner Alliance (NZAOA), bringing together asset managers to collaborate on increasing the number of blended-finance vehicles serving EMDEs (NZAOA 2021). NZAOA is an initiative of institutional investors committed to transitioning their investment portfolios to net zero GHG emissions by 2050 and an important member of GFANZ.

To promote blended finance more extensively, it is important to address information asymmetry problems between recipients and creditors and investors, which tend to be severe in EMDEs (Shirai 2022a, 2022b). Currently, most ESG investment occurs in developed countries, where capital and financial markets are well developed and numerous issuers and investors are required to disclose audited financial statements. This situation does not necessarily apply to many EMDEs. A blended finance mechanism, therefore, might need to allocate a larger share of public funds at the initial phase while private investors invest smaller amounts. Private investors can provide an increased share of funding at a later phase after the project becomes more viable. Blended finance is important because blending the public fund portion with private funding can attract additional private funding for projects that otherwise would not have been possible. With the participation of project developers and private companies—as well as well-experienced multilateral and/or bilateral development finance banks, charitable foundations, and nongovernment organizations—blended finance is able to reduce the information asymmetry faced by investors.

Convergence, a nonprofit organization, publishes a report on trends with the aim of developing the global blended finance market. Convergence classifies blended finance schemes

continued on next page

Box 2 *continued*

into four types, as shown in **Figure B2.2** (Convergence 2021). In the Type 1 Scheme (Catalytic Funds), public funds and charitable foundations contribute the riskiest portion of equity capital to absorb first losses in the event of failure. Under the Type 2 Scheme (Guarantees or Insurance), public funds or foundations provide partial or full guarantees, or provide insurance at below market terms, thereby reducing the foreign exchange and political risks faced by private investors. In the Type 3 Scheme (Technical Assistance), developed countries provide technical assistance to support the formulation of project design in the initial stage and to assist project and fund managers after investment. The Type 4 Scheme (Grants) aims at accelerating the initiation of a project by providing grants at the stage of project design and preparation, and the creation of a financing system.

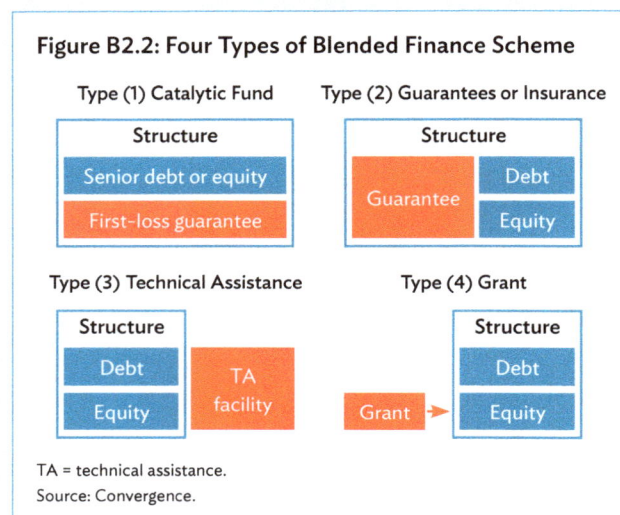

Figure B2.2: Four Types of Blended Finance Scheme

TA = technical assistance.
Source: Convergence.

Among the four types, Type 1 is the most frequently utilized scheme, accounting for 85% of blended finance in 2020. This share rose in 2020 from the previous year partly because the risk of investing in EMDEs increased with the onset of the COVID-19 pandemic, indicating that it became more difficult to mobilize private capital without the catalytic effect of the funding being enhanced. Type 2 also has the effect of reducing risk for private investors, but it is not yet fully utilized perhaps because there are few public finance institutions that provide guarantees. Type 3 was the second-most utilized scheme in 2020.

In recent years, some blended finance initiatives have emerged as a result of joint efforts among developed countries. For example, developed countries formed the Just Energy Transition Partnerships (JETPs) for South Africa (USD8.5 billion) in 2021, Indonesia (USD20.0 billion) and Viet Nam (USD15.5 billion) in 2022, and Senegal (EUR2.8 billion) in 2023. For most JETP schemes, the pledged amounts will be shared equally by developed countries (including the European Union, France, Germany Japan, the United Kingdom, and the United States) and financial institutions. The GFANZ working group, comprising banks and institutional investors, supports the JETPs.

More countries, especially smaller and/or low-income countries, should be given access to such jointly managed funds. Moreover, these funding pledges may not represent additional or new finance being provided to EMDEs, and thus they can end up diverting from other important projects and other countries. Further, developed countries' pledges have traditionally been hard to fulfill, resulting in disparities between commitments and actual disbursements (Liao and Beal 2022). It is even more uncertain whether sufficient funds from financial institutions can be collected to meet the pledged financing amounts.

Given the limited budgetary resources available in EMDEs, developed countries collectively need to explore how to maximize the effectiveness of public funds by mobilizing more private capital inflows. For example, the important role of catalytic funds in blended finance should be more actively discussed by the Group of Seven and Group of Twenty to increase collaboration. The idea of shifting some grants included in official development assistance toward catalytic funds or equity tranches with joint contributions from developed countries should be examined as well. In addition, more priority can be placed on increasing the contributions of public and private capital to the specialized multilateral climate and environmental funds that promote blended finance for EMDEs (Shirai 2022a). These funds include the United Nations-led Green Climate Fund and are often intermediated through multilateral development banks or bilateral development institutions, which are able to promote climate projects and attract institutional investors by forming catalytic funds in a transparent and efficient manner.

continued on next page

Box 2 *continued*

References

Convergence. 2021. *The State of Blended Finance 2021*. Toronto.

International Energy Agency. 2021. *Financing Clean Energy Transitions in Emerging and Developing Economies*. June. https://www.convergence.finance/resource/the-state-of-blended-finance-2021/view.

Liao, C. Liang and T. Beal. 2022. "The Role of the G7 in Mobilizing for Global Recovery." Chatham House Research Paper. https://www.chathamhouse.org/sites/default/files/2022-06/2022-06-24-role-g7-mobilizing-global-recovery-liao-beal.pdf.

Net-Zero Asset Owner Alliance. 2021. *Alliance Climate Blended Finance Vehicles' Call to Action to Asset Managers*. https://www.unepfi.org/wordpress/wp-content/uploads/2022/03/NZAOA-Renewed-Call-to-Action-to-Asset-Managers.pdf.

Organisation for Economic Co-operation and Development. 2022. *Climate Finance Provided and Mobilised by Developed Countries in 2016–2020: Insights from Disaggregated Analysis*. Paris: OECD Publishing. https://www.oecd.org/environment/climate-finance-provided-and-mobilised-by-developed-countries-in-2016-2020-286dae5d-en.htm.

Shirai, S. 2022a. "An Overview on Climate Environment, and Innovative Finance in Emerging and Developing Economies." Asian Development Bank Institute Working Paper Series 1347. https://www.adb.org/publications/an-overview-of-climate-change-the-environment-and-innovative-finance-in-emerging-and-developing-economies.

———. 2022b. "Promoting Innovative Climate Finance in Emerging and Developing Economies." *ADBI Asian Pathways*. 14 December.

Policy and Regulatory Developments

People's Republic of China

People's Bank of China Extends Support to the Real Estate Sector

On 10 July, the People's Bank of China announced that it would extend the duration of some support measures for real estate companies that were passed on 11 November 2022. The two measures to be extended are (i) delaying repayments of loans availed by real estate companies by 1 year, and (ii) not making adjustments for the risk classifications of real estate companies for the duration of the loans provided.

People's Bank of China Raises Macroprudential Adjustment Parameter

On 20 July, the People's Bank of China, together with the State Administration of Foreign Exchange, raised the macroprudential adjustment parameter from 1.25 to 1.50 for cross-border financing. The macroprudential adjustment parameter forms part of the calculation that determines the maximum amount of cross-border financing that enterprises and financial institutions can have outstanding.

Hong Kong, China

Hong Kong Monetary Authority Maintains Countercyclical Capital Buffer Ratio at 1.0%

On 13 July, the Hong Kong Monetary Authority (HKMA) announced that the countercyclical buffer (CCyB) ratio remained unchanged at 1.0%. The HKMA stated that economic activities had further stabilized and the latest indicators based on data from the first quarter of 2023 signaled a CCyB of 0.0%. Considering the elevated level of uncertainty in the global environment, the HKMA decided to hold the CCyB at 1.0%. The CCyB is an integral part of the Basel III regulatory capital framework intended to improve the resilience of the banking sector.

Indonesia

Ministry of Finance to Lower Debt Issuance Plan

In May, the Ministry of Finance disclosed plans to reduce bond issuance for the remainder of the year as the Government of Indonesia posted a budget surplus amid increased revenue collection. The government also plans to use excess cash generated in 2022 to help reduce bond offerings. In July, the government subsequently announced that net bond issuance is estimated to be cut to IDR362.9 trillion from the original target of IDR712.9 trillion. The reduced bond offerings were based on new assumptions presented at a parliamentary hearing that included a reduced budget deficit in 2023 equivalent to a gross domestic product share of 2.28%, down from 2.84% as initially estimated.

Republic of Korea

The Republic of Korea Announces Economic Policy Directions for the Second Half of 2023

On 4 July, the Government of the Republic of Korea announced its economic policy directions for the second half of 2023. Economic growth is projected to be 1.4%, which is less than the initial forecast, but it is expected to improve in the second half of the year due to the recovery in the information technology industry. The government will focus on (i) enhancing economic vitality, which includes providing financial support to facilitate a rebound in exports, among other measures; (ii) providing price stability to support the reduction of living expenses, particularly utility costs, agricultural products, and housing costs; (iii) improving fundamental economic structures, which includes funding science and technology and high-tech industries, and structural reforms in labor, education, and national pensions; and (iv) addressing future challenges such as low birth rates, an aging population, and the climate and energy crises.

Malaysia

Bank Negara Malaysia Intervenes in the Foreign Exchange Market

On 27 June, Bank Negara Malaysia's Financial Markets Committee announced that the central bank would intervene in the foreign exchange market to ensure that the value of the Malaysian ringgit properly reflects the fundamentals of the Malaysian economy. The committee clarified that the recent depreciation of the ringgit against the United States dollar was driven by investor expectations of higher interest rates in major economies, while the ringgit's depreciation against the Chinese yuan could be attributed to the People's Republic of China being one of the biggest trading partners of Malaysia. The Financial Markets Committee assessed that in 2023 Malaysia is expected to continue its strong growth momentum from the previous year. Further, the committee noted that the volatility of the ringgit's exchange rate is low compared to other regional currencies and foreign holdings of Malaysian government securities remain close to the long-term average. Although the ringgit's exchange rate is driven by external factors, the central bank is confident that expected economic growth and fiscal policies of Malaysia will continue to support the currency.

Philippines

Bangko Sentral ng Pilipinas Starts 56-Day Bill Offering

Effective 30 June, the Bangko Sentral ng Pilipinas (BSP) began selling 56-day BSP bills as an additional tenor under the BSP Securities Facility alongside the 28-day BSP bill. The newly launched central bank bill improves the BSP's adaptability to shifting liquidity conditions and provides additional guidance to short-term market interest rates. The introduction of the new central bank bill supports the government's initiatives in promoting more flexible and market-based liquidity management in the financial system.

Bangko Sentral ng Pilipinas Lowers Reserve Requirement Ratio

On 8 June, the BSP reduced the reserve requirement ratio by 250 basis points (bps) for banks and non-bank financial institutions to 9.5%, effective 30 June. The cut aims to ensure stability in domestic liquidity and credit conditions, and address any rate tightening effects on banks' liquidity positions once the pandemic-related measures expire. Reserve requirement ratios for digital banks and rural and cooperative banks were also lowered by 200 bps and 100 bps, respectively.

Singapore

Central Banks of Singapore and Cambodia to Expand Support for Small and Medium-Sized Enterprises

On 11 July, the Monetary Authority of Singapore and the National Bank of Cambodia agreed to develop a Financial Transparency Corridor (FTC). The scheme aspires to create digital infrastructure that allows intra-regional transactions between small and medium-sized enterprises (SMEs) in Singapore and Cambodia. Financial institutions from the two economies will be able to obtain trusted information conveniently from Singaporean and Cambodian SMEs through the FTC for the purpose of providing financial services to a buyer transacting with a seller from the other economy. Aside from supporting SMEs, the FTC can also help develop better products and services between Singapore and Cambodia.

Thailand

Bank of Thailand Plans Further Easing of Foreign Exchange Regulations

On 27 June, the Bank of Thailand (BOT) announced plans to further ease foreign exchange rules to help individuals and companies manage exchange rate risks. The BOT foresees that the Thai baht will remain volatile in the short run due to external factors. The central bank will double the threshold for direct overseas investment in equities for individuals to USD10 million annually. The BOT will also raise the amount allowed for cross-border money transfers from USD50,000 to USD200,000. Furthermore, the central bank will relax the rules for Thai units of foreign companies to send money to parent companies, a process known as "notional pooling." The measures are scheduled to be implemented starting in the third quarter of 2023.

Viet Nam

Corporate Bond Trading System Goes Live

On 19 July, Hanoi Stock Exchange launched the new trading platform for privately issued corporate bonds. The system enables investors to trade bonds on the stock exchange almost like normal stocks, but in a T+0 payment mechanism where money and bonds will be immediately credited to investors' accounts. In addition, trading sessions of corporate bonds are scheduled separately on the stock exchange, from Monday to Friday each week lasting from 9 am to 11:30 am and from 1 pm to 2:45 pm, excluding public holidays. The launch of the trading platform will give new impetus to the corporate bond market by improving its liquidity, transparency, and better access to capital.

Central Bank Issues New Circulars on Debt Payment Rescheduling and Bond Repurchases by Banks

On 23 April, the State Bank of Vietnam issued Circular Nos. 2 and 3 to support businesses, particularly the real estate market, and broaden the economy's credit operations. Circular No. 2 provides guidelines for banks on debt rescheduling and the retention of debt categories for loans and leased finance. Effective 24 April until 30 June 2024, banks can restructure repayment terms for distressed customers by not classifying them as nonperforming loans but instead requiring at least 50% additional loan loss provision until the end of this year and 100% until the end of 2024. Circular No. 2 aims to ease the pressure of debt repayments for borrowers by allowing new credits or refinancing for qualified customers. Meanwhile, Circular No. 3 suspended the validity of Clause 11 Article 4 of Circular No. 16 (dated 10 November 2021) from 24 April 2023 to 31 December 2023. The new circular allows credit institutions and foreign bank branches to immediately repurchase unlisted corporate bonds with the highest internal credit ratings without waiting 12 months after selling. Circular No. 3 aims to stabilize market sentiments among issuers and investors, increase liquidity, and strengthen the recovery of the corporate bond market.

Market Summaries

People's Republic of China

Yield Movements

Between 1 June and 31 August, local currency (LCY) government bond yields in the People's Republic of China (PRC) declined for most maturities after a series of interest rate cuts intended to spur economic growth (**Figure 1**). The People's Bank of China (PBOC) reduced the 7-day reverse repo rate by 10 basis points (bps) to 1.90% on 13 June, which was followed by a 10 bps reduction of the 1-year medium-term lending facility rate to 2.65% on 15 June. On 20 June, the PBOC reduced the 1-year loan prime rate and the 5-year loan prime rate by 10 bps each to 3.55% and 4.20%, respectively. On 15 August, the PBOC reduced again the 1-year medium-term lending rate by 15 bps to 2.50% and the 7-day reverse repo rate by 10 bps to 1.80%. It also reduced by 10 bps the 1-year loan prime rate to 3.45% on 21 August.

In addition, the PRC unveiled a series of property easing measures. These include an extension of some measures enacted last November 2022 to December 2024 in June, as well as a reduction in interest rates on existing mortgages and lower downpayments on home purchases in August. This was done to support the flagging property sector that has been hit by a number of defaults, with Sino-Ocean and Country Garden Holdings among the most recent.

Local Currency Bond Market Size and Issuance

The PRC's LCY bonds outstanding grew at a slightly slower pace as the government maintained its issuance levels in the second quarter (Q2) of 2023 to provide economic support (**Figure 2**). LCY bonds outstanding in the PRC grew 2.0% quarter-on-quarter (q-o-q) to CNY132.9 trillion at the end of Q2 2023. Government bonds outstanding grew 2.4% q-o-q to CNY87.9 trillion, with growth largely driven by local government bonds as local governments continued to issue to meet their targeted bond quotas by the end of the third quarter of 2023. Corporate bonds outstanding grew 1.2% q-o-q to CNY44.9 trillion.

Figure 2: Composition of Local Currency Bonds Outstanding in the People's Republic of China

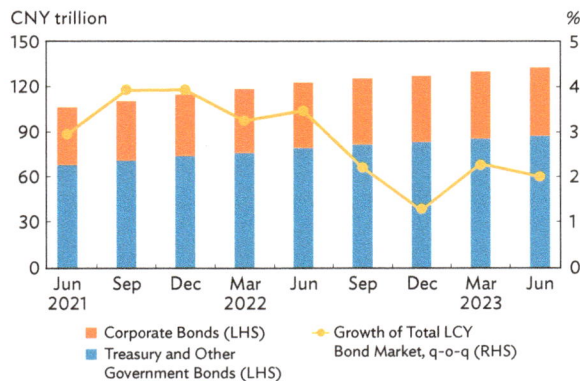

CNY = Chinese yuan, LCY = local currency, LHS = left-hand side, q-o-q = quarter-on-quarter, RHS = right-hand side.
Source: CEIC Data Company.

Figure 1: The People's Republic of China's Benchmark Yield Curve—Local Currency Government Bonds

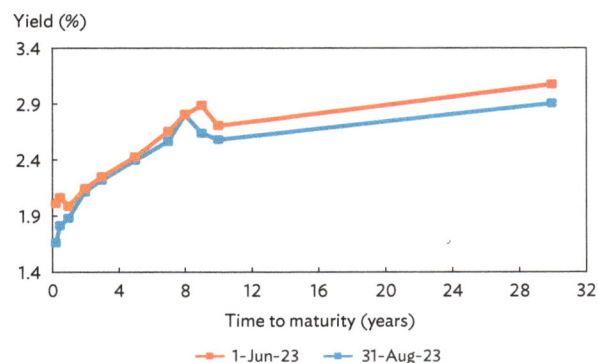

Source: Based on data from Bloomberg LP.

LCY bond sales in the PRC totaled CNY10.8 trillion in Q2 2023, growing 6.5% q-o-q on increased issuance of both government and corporate bonds (Figure 3). Issuance of Treasury and other government bonds climbed 2.7% q-o-q in Q2 2023 after local governments received their new yearly bond quotas for full-year 2023. Issuance of corporate bonds gained as financial institutions replenished their capital and funding needs in Q2 2023.

Investor Profile

Commercial banks remained the largest investor group in the government bond market at the end of June (Figure 4). Commercial banks maintained their lead as the dominant holder of government bonds with a share of nearly 80.0% for all government bonds outstanding at the end of June. Commercial banks also held the largest share of local government bonds at the end of June with 78.8%.

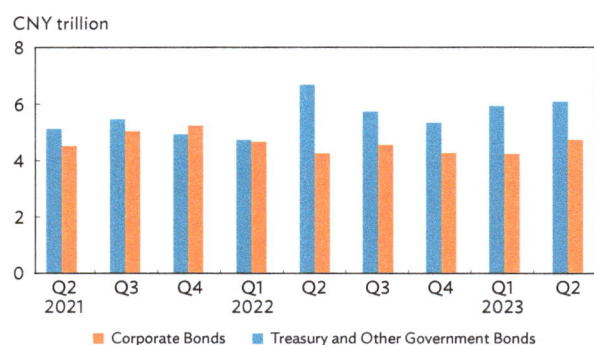

Figure 3: Composition of Local Currency Bond Issuance in the People's Republic of China

CNY = Chinese yuan, Q1 = first quarter, Q2 = second quarter, Q3 = third quarter, Q4 = fourth quarter.
Source: CEIC Data Company.

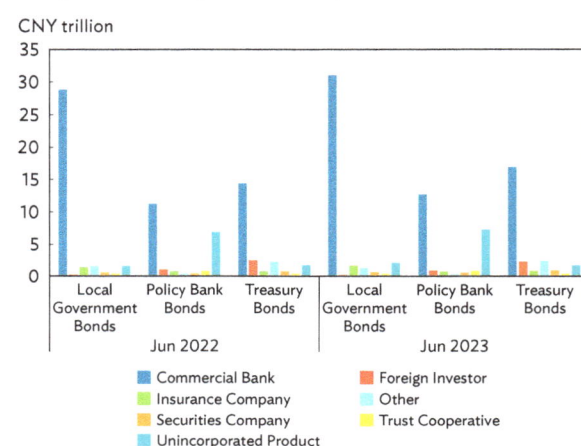

Figure 4: Investor Profile of Local Government Bonds, Policy Bank Bonds, and Treasury Bonds

CNY = Chinese yuan.
Source: CEIC Data Company.

Hong Kong, China

Yield Movements

Between 1 June and 31 August, Hong Kong, China's local currency (LCY) bond yields showed mixed movements (Figure 1). Yields fell for bonds with maturities of less than 1 year, but rose for bonds with maturities of 1 year or longer. The decline in short-term yields was influenced by market expectations of a pause in the United States (US) Federal Reserve's rate hikes at its upcoming September meeting amid easing inflation in the US. Consumer price inflation in Hong Kong, China also decelerated to 1.8% year-on-year (y-o-y) in July from 1.9% y-o-y in June and 2.0% y-o-y in May. Meanwhile, the rise in yields for medium- to longer-term bonds was mostly driven by elevated interest rates due to the Federal Reserve's previous monetary policy tightening and the Hong Kong Monetary Authority's (HKMA) consequent rate hikes. The HKMA raised its base rate by 25 bps to a record high of 5.75% on 27 July after the Federal Reserve raised interest rates by 25 bps to a range of 5.25%–5.50% during its 25–26 July meeting. The HKMA adjusts its base rate in lockstep with Federal Reserve monetary policy changes to maintain the Hong Kong dollar's peg to the US dollar.

Local Currency Bond Market Size and Issuance

Hong Kong, China's LCY bond market reached a size of HKD2.9 trillion at the end of June (Figure 2). Growth in Hong Kong, China's LCY bond market picked up 2.4% quarter-on-quarter (q-o-q) in the second quarter (Q2) of 2023, driven in part by a rebound in the issuance of Hong Kong Special Administrative Region (HKSAR) government bonds. LCY corporate bonds outstanding totaled HKD1.4 trillion at the end of June, representing nearly half of total outstanding LCY bonds. Outstanding Exchange Fund Bills and Exchange Fund Notes (HKD1.2 trillion) and HKSAR government bonds (HKD234.5 billion) comprised the remaining 42.8% and 8.2%, respectively, of Hong Kong, China's LCY bond market.

Figure 1: Hong Kong, China's Benchmark Yield Curve— Exchange Fund Bills and Notes

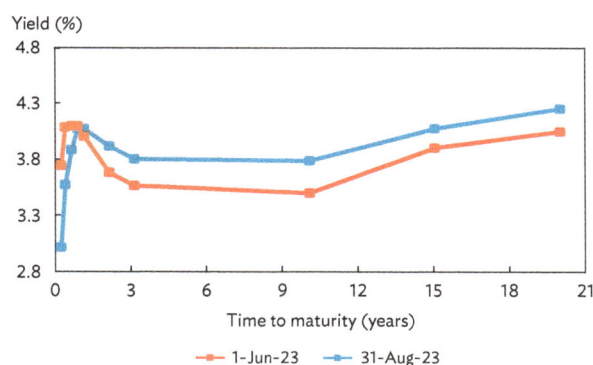

Source: Based on data from Bloomberg LP.

Figure 2: Composition of Local Currency Bonds Outstanding in Hong Kong, China

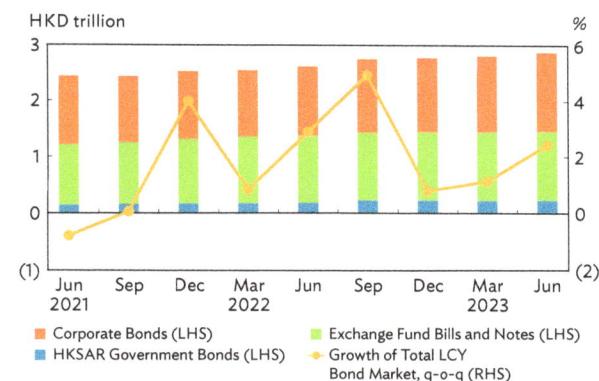

( ) = negative, HKD = Hong Kong dollar, HKSAR = Hong Kong Special Administrative Region, LCY = local currency, LHS = left-hand side, q-o-q = quarter-on-quarter, RHS = right-hand side.
Source: Hong Kong Monetary Authority.

Issuance of LCY bonds in Hong Kong, China contracted in Q2 2023, driven by a decline in corporate debt issuance (Figure 3). Issuance of new corporate bonds fell 22.9% q-o-q to HKD214.3 billion in Q2 2023 amid elevated borrowing costs. Hong Kong Mortgage Corporation continued to be the largest nonbank issuer of LCY corporate bonds, with total issuances worth HKD17.9 billion in Q2 2023. Meanwhile, new issuance of HKSAR government bonds tallied HKD9.5 billion in Q2 2023, up 21.8% from Q1 2023 due to a relatively large issuance (HKD5.0 billion) of 3-year bonds in April.

Hong Kong, China raised USD6.0 billion worth of multicurrency green bonds in June. The issuance—denominated in US dollars, euros, and Chinese yuan—met strong demand with almost USD30 billion equivalent in orders. Increased access through Southbound Bond Connect supported significant participation from international investors. The triple-currency issuance comprised USD2.3 billion, EUR1.5 billion, and CNY15.0 billion worth of bonds with maturities of 2–10 years. Compared to a similar triple-currency green bond issuance in January, the June green bond issuance had a larger share of CNY-denominated bonds, as the Chinese yuan tranche was expanded to include a 10-year green bond to cater to investor demand and extend the offshore Chinese yuan yield curve (**Figure 4**). Hong Kong, China continues to develop its green bond portfolio to promote sustainable finance.

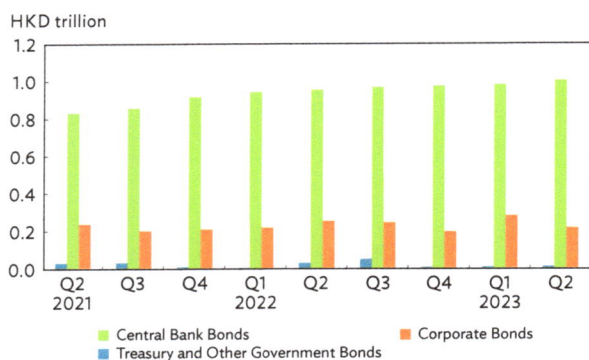

Figure 3: Composition of Local Currency Bond Issuance in Hong Kong, China

HKD = Hong Kong dollar, Q1 = first quarter, Q2 = second quarter, Q3 = third quarter, Q4 = fourth quarter.
Source: Hong Kong Monetary Authority.

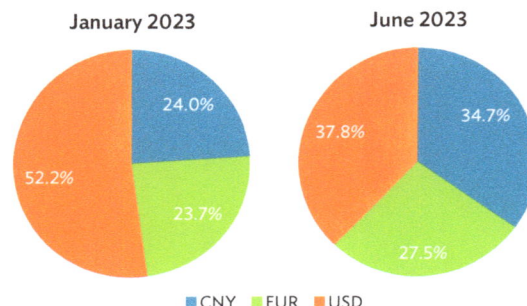

Figure 4: Currency Breakdown of Institutional Green Bond Issuance in Hong Kong, China

CNY = Chinese yuan, EUR = euro, USD = United States dollar.
Note: Figures were computed based on 30 June 2023 currency exchange rates and do not include currency effects.
Source: *AsianBondsOnline* calculations based on Hong Kong Monetary Authority data.

Indonesia

Yield Movements

Between 1 June and 31 August, local currency (LCY) government bond yields in Indonesia rose for most tenors. Bond yields climbed for most maturities of 10 years or less but fell for longer-end tenors (12 years or more) during the review period (**Figure 1**). The uptick in yields for most tenors was driven by the continued monetary tightening stance of the United States Federal Reserve. Also pressuring yields were expectations that Bank Indonesia would hold rates steady for the rest of the year. In contrast, yields declined at the long-end of the curve as inflation returned to within the central bank's target range of 2.0%–4.0% in May, which was earlier than previously projected. Bank Indonesia remains confident inflation will stay within the target range for the rest of the year.

Local Currency Bond Market Size and Issuance

The LCY bond market in Indonesia contracted in the second quarter (Q2) of 2023 due to a slowdown in both government and corporate bond issuances. Indonesia's outstanding bonds dropped 0.5% quarter-on-quarter (q-o-q), amounting to IDR6,130.6 trillion compared with the previous quarter's total of IDR6,161.1 trillion (**Figure 2**). Outstanding government bonds dipped 0.5% q-o-q to IDR5,632.9 trillion as the government tapered its planned bond issuances for the year amid expected higher revenue collections. The government also plans to use excess cash generated from 2022 to partially fund fiscal spending for 2023. The stock of corporate bonds declined on a q-o-q basis as maturities exceeded issuances. Corporate bond issuance in Q2 2023 declined 41.3% q-o-q (IDR16.1 trillion) amid reduced refinancing needs by corporates as interest rates remained elevated.

Figure 1: Indonesia's Benchmark Yield Curve—Local Currency Government Bonds

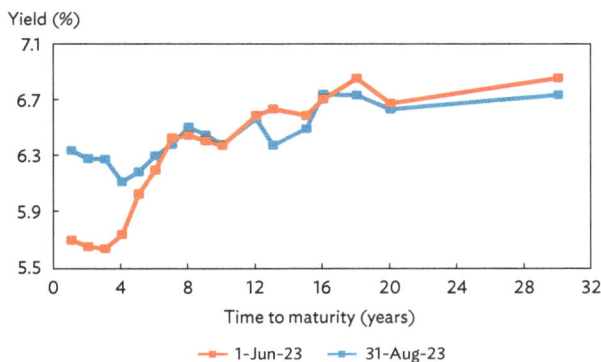

Source: Based on data from Bloomberg LP.

Figure 2: Composition of Local Currency Bonds Outstanding in Indonesia

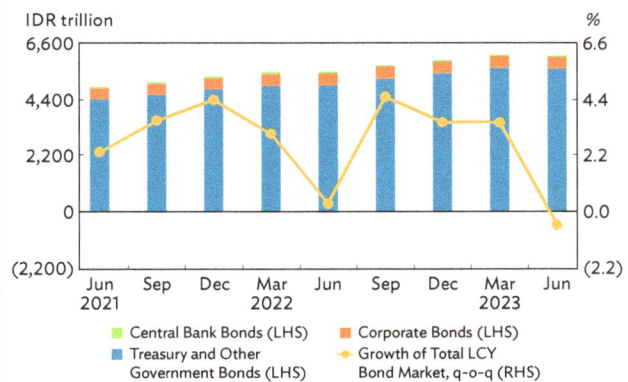

( ) = negative, IDR = Indonesian rupiah, LCY = local currency, LHS = left-hand side, q-o-q = quarter-on-quarter, RHS = right-hand side.

Note: Data includes *sukuk* (Islamic bonds). Data for Treasury and other government bonds comprised of tradable and nontradable central government bonds.

Sources: Bank Indonesia; Directorate General of Budget Financing and Risk Management, Ministry of Finance; and Indonesia Stock Exchange.

LCY bond issuance slowed in Q2 2023, posting q-o-q contractions across all bond types (Figure 3). Total bond issuance fell 35.7% q-o-q to IDR349.8 trillion. Treasury bond issuance, which accounted for 43.4% of total LCY bond issuance during the quarter, declined 38.1% q-o-q after the government had frontloaded funding in the prior quarter. Corporate bond issuance also slowed by 41.3% q-o-q, with only 12 firms tapping the bond market for fundraising versus 21 companies in the preceding quarter. Corporate bond issuance in Q2 2023 was dominated by financing companies, with the largest issuances coming from Sarana Multi Infrastruktur, BFI Finance Indonesia, and Pegadaian. Meanwhile, central bank bond issuance declined amid slowing inflation.

Investor Profile

Domestic investors collectively accounted for 84.5% of the total tradable central government bonds at the end of June, up from 83.9% in the same period a year earlier. Similar with its emerging East Asian peers, banking institutions were the largest investor group in Indonesia's LCY bond market, collectively adding IDR263.2 trillion worth of government bonds to their holdings in Q2 2023 from the prior year (**Figure 4**). However, unlike regional peers, central bank holdings of government bonds in Indonesia are quite substantial, making it the second-largest domestic investor group. Bank Indonesia's holdings of government bonds significantly rose during the pandemic period as part of macroprudential measures to support bond market stability.

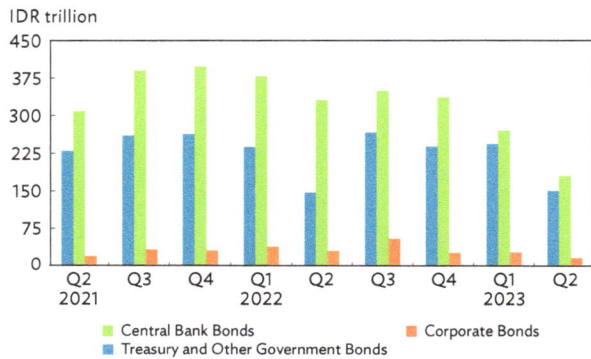

Figure 3: Composition of Local Currency Bond Issuance in Indonesia

IDR trillion

IDR = Indonesian rupiah, Q1 = first quarter, Q2 = second quarter, Q3 = third quarter, Q4 = fourth quarter.

Note: Data includes *sukuk* (Islamic bonds). Data for Treasury and other government bonds comprise tradable and nontradable central government bonds.

Sources: Bank Indonesia; Directorate General of Budget Financing and Risk Management, Ministry of Finance; and Indonesia Stock Exchange.

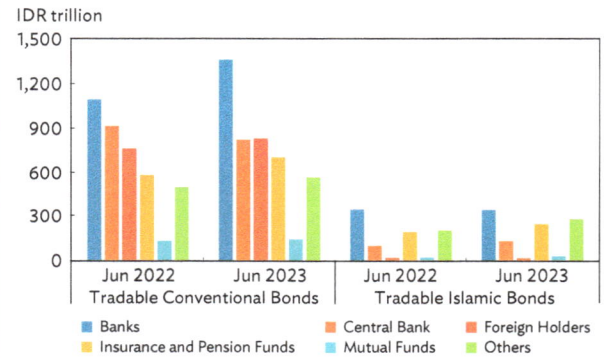

Figure 4: Investor Profile of Tradable Central Government Bonds

IDR trillion

IDR = Indonesian rupiah.

Source: Directorate General of Budget Financing and Risk Management, Ministry of Finance.

Republic of Korea

Yield Movements

The Republic of Korea's local currency (LCY) government bond yields rose for most tenors between 1 June and 31 August, tracking the rise in United States Treasury yields on continued Federal Reserve monetary tightening and solid economic conditions (Figure 1). Upward pressure on yields also stemmed from expectations that the Bank of Korea (BOK) will keep the base rate at 3.50% in the near term as it forecasts inflation to start picking up again. In its 13 July and 24 August monetary policy meetings, the BOK stated that although inflation has slowed, it is expected to rise again and remain above the target level for a considerable time. Also in its August monetary policy meeting, the BOK maintained its May inflation forecasts for 2023 and 2024 at 3.5% year-on-year (y-o-y) and 2.4% y-o-y, respectively. Moreover, the growth forecast for 2023 was maintained at 1.4% y-o-y, while that for 2024 was lowered to 2.2% y-o-y from 2.3% y-o-y.

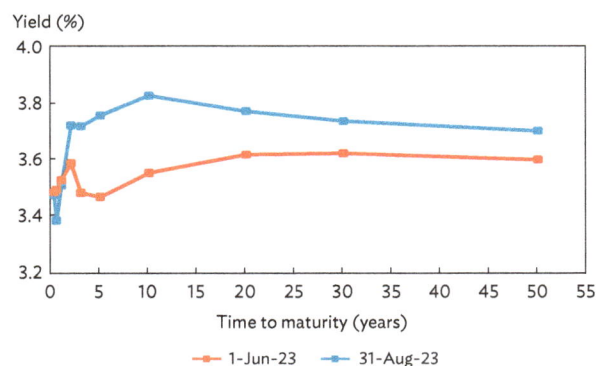

Figure 1: The Republic of Korea's Benchmark Yield Curve—Local Currency Government Bonds

Yield (%)

— 1-Jun-23   — 31-Aug-23

Source: Based on data from Bloomberg LP.

Local Currency Bond Market Size and Issuance

The Republic of Korea's LCY bonds outstanding grew 2.6% quarter-on-quarter (q-o-q) in the second quarter (Q2) of 2023, driven by both the government and corporate bond segments. The Republic of Korea's

LCY bond market reached a size of KRW3,092.6 trillion at the end of June. Corporate bonds, which comprise over half of the total LCY bond market, posted growth of 2.7% q-o-q in Q2 2023, up from 1.3% q-o-q in the first quarter (Q1) of 2023, due to a rebound in issuance during the quarter (**Figure 2**). The stock of Treasury and other government bonds increased 2.5% q-o-q to KRW1,191.2 trillion, exceeding the 1.2% q-o-q growth posted in Q1 2023. Treasury and other government bonds accounted for 38.5% of the Republic of Korea's LCY bond market at the end of June, unchanged from its share in Q1 2023.

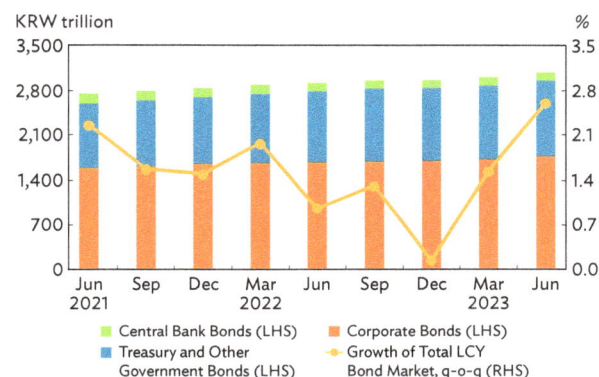

Figure 2: Composition of Local Currency Bonds Outstanding in the Republic of Korea

KRW trillion   %

- Central Bank Bonds (LHS)
- Corporate Bonds (LHS)
- Treasury and Other Government Bonds (LHS)
- Growth of Total LCY Bond Market, q-o-q (RHS)

KRW = Korean won, LCY = local currency, LHS = left-hand side, q-o-q = quarter-on-quarter, RHS = right-hand side.

Sources: Bank of Korea and KG Zeroin Corp.

Total LCY bond issuance jumped 26.6% q-o-q to KRW312.9 trillion in Q2 2023, up from 4.7% q-o-q in Q1 2023, driven by higher issuance volumes in both the corporate and government bond market segments. Corporate bond issuance rebounded in Q2 2023, posting a 28.0% q-o-q increase in Q2 2023, following a 6.2% q-o-q contraction in Q1 2023 (**Figure 3**). The gains were led by the higher quarterly issuance volumes of private companies and financial debentures. Firms also took advantage of the favorable environment to issue bonds in anticipation of a rise in yields as the Federal Reserve was expected to implement another set of rate hikes before the end of the year. One of the largest corporate bond issuances

Figure 3: Composition of Local Currency Bond Issuance in the Republic of Korea

KRW trillion

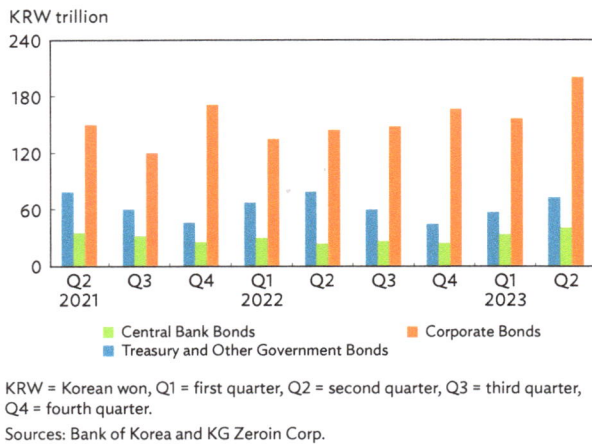

KRW = Korean won, Q1 = first quarter, Q2 = second quarter, Q3 = third quarter, Q4 = fourth quarter.
Sources: Bank of Korea and KG Zeroin Corp.

Figure 4: Local Currency Bonds Outstanding Investor Profile

%

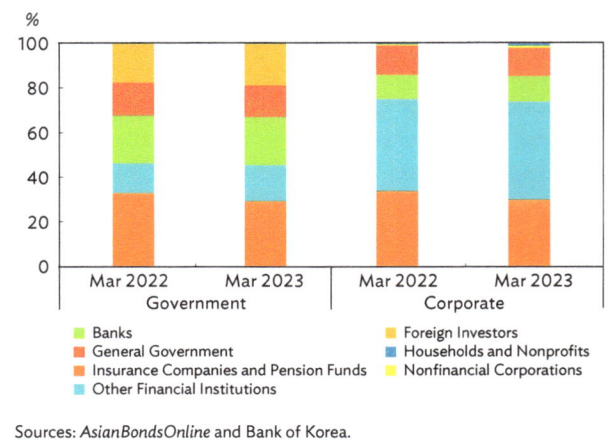

Sources: *AsianBondsOnline* and Bank of Korea.

in Q2 2023 was the KRW1.0 trillion multitranche bond issued by LG Energy Solutions in June. Issuance of Treasury and other government bonds posted rapid growth of 27.2% q-o-q in Q2 2023. The Government of the Republic of Korea continued to issue a high volume of Treasury bonds during the quarter to fund its frontloading policy of expending 65% of its 2023 budget in the first half of the year to help prop up the economy.

Investor Profile

Insurance companies and pension funds continued to hold the largest share of the Republic of Korea's LCY bonds outstanding at the end of March. The investor group held 29.4% of government bonds outstanding at the end of Q1 2023, which reflected a decline from its share of 33.0% a year earlier (**Figure 4**). Banks were the second-largest investor group with a share of 21.6%, while the share of foreign investors rose to 18.6% from 17.2% during the same period. In the corporate bond market, other financial institutions were the largest investor group with a share of 43.9%, followed by insurance companies and pension funds at 30.0%. The foreign holdings share of LCY corporate bonds remained negligible at 0.4% at the end of March.

Foreign investors returned to the Republic of Korea's LCY bond market in Q2 2023. Aggregate net foreign bond inflows reached a record high of KRW17.6 trillion in Q2 2023, a reversal from the KRW4.3 trillion of net bond outflows in Q1 2023 and the highest quarterly net

Figure 5: Net Foreign Investment in Local Currency Bonds in the Republic of Korea by Remaining Maturity

KRW trillion

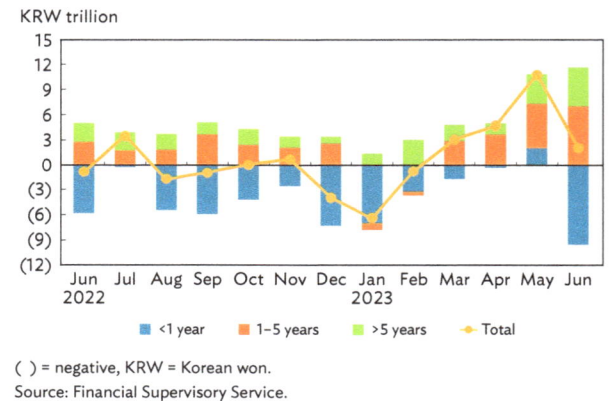

( ) = negative, KRW = Korean won.
Source: Financial Supervisory Service.

bond inflows since Q2 2021. Net foreign bond inflows to the Republic of Korea's LCY bond market totaled KRW15.6 trillion in April and May as market participants were expecting the Bank of Korea to cut its policy rate before the end of the year due to slowing domestic inflation and the Federal Reserve continuing to ease the pace of its monetary policy tightening (**Figure 5**). In June, however, net foreign bond inflows slowed to KRW2.1 trillion following a Bank of Korea statement on 8 June that it would continue its current monetary policy as upward pressure on inflation remained. Foreign demand declined as the Bank of Korea's statement was seen as lowering the chance of another rate cut this year.

Malaysia

Yield Movements

The local currency (LCY) government bond yield curve of Malaysia shifted upward between 1 June and 31 August (Figure 1). The yield curve's movement largely tracked that of the United States (US), whose Treasury bond yields increased for all tenors during the review period. On 6 July, Bank Negara Malaysia decided to keep its overnight policy rate unchanged at 3.00% after a surprise 25-basis-points rate hike on 3 May. Investors remain cautious as the US Federal Reserve hiked its interest rates during its July meeting to contain consumer price inflation and maintain a high employment rate.

Figure 2: Composition of Local Currency Bonds Outstanding in Malaysia

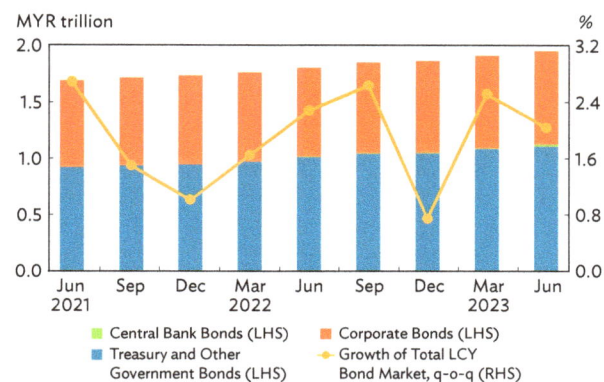

LCY = local currency, LHS = left-hand side, MYR = Malaysian ringgit, q-o-q = quarter-on-quarter, RHS = right-hand side.
Source: Bank Negara Malaysia Fully Automated System for Issuing/Tendering.

Figure 1: Malaysia's Benchmark Yield Curve— Local Currency Government Bonds

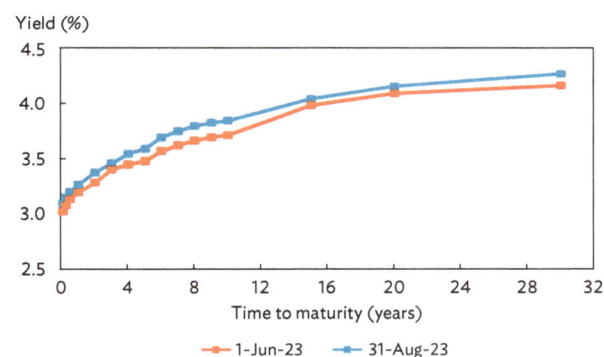

Source: Based on data from Bloomberg LP.

Local Currency Bond Market Size and Issuance

The LCY bond market of Malaysia expanded 2.0% to reach MYR1,953.1 billion in the second quarter (Q2) of 2023 on increased outstanding securities for all LCY bond types (Figure 2). Fixed-income securities of the Government of Malaysia remained the main drivers of expansion in the Malaysian LCY bond market. Treasury and other government securities outstanding grew, albeit at a slower pace compared to the first quarter (Q1) of 2023, due to reduced issuance during the review period. Partially contributing to the LCY bond market's growth was a continued increase in outstanding Bank Negara Malaysia bills, which constituted just 0.6%

of total LCY bonds. In Q2 2023, outstanding corporate bonds also jumped. DanaInfra Nasional, a government-owned finance company, continued to be the top corporate bond issuer at the end of June 2023, with total LCY bonds outstanding totaling MYR82.9 billion.

Issuance of LCY bonds in Malaysia rebounded in Q2 2023, rising 12.1% quarter-on-quarter (q-o-q) due to increased issuance from the central bank and corporate entities (Figure 3). This expansion was slightly offset by a decline in the issuance of Treasury and other government bonds. Malaysian Government Securities (conventional bonds) issuance dipped 10.0% q-o-q, while the issuance of Government Investment Issues (*sukuk*, or Islamic bonds) was steady from the previous quarter. During the quarter, Cagamas, or the National Mortgage Corporation of Malaysia, was the leading issuer in the market with seven issuances of Islamic commercial paper, five *sukuk*, and nine conventional bonds all totaling MYR6.1 billion.

In Q2 2023, 64.1% of Malaysia's LCY bonds outstanding were Islamic bonds (Figure 4). Outstanding Islamic bonds totaled MYR1.3 trillion at the end of June, equivalent to growth of 2.3% q-o-q. Comprising most of the outstanding LCY corporate bonds, corporate *sukuk* continued to drive the Islamic bond market's growth in Q2 2023.

Figure 3: Composition of Local Currency Bond Issuance in Malaysia

MYR billion

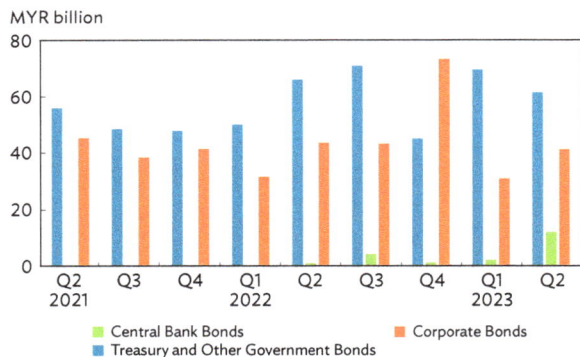

MYR = Malaysian ringgit, Q1 = first quarter, Q2 = second quarter, Q3 = third quarter, Q4 = fourth quarter.
Source: Bank Negara Malaysia Fully Automated System for Issuing/Tendering.

Figure 4: Composition of Local Currency Islamic Bonds Outstanding in Malaysia

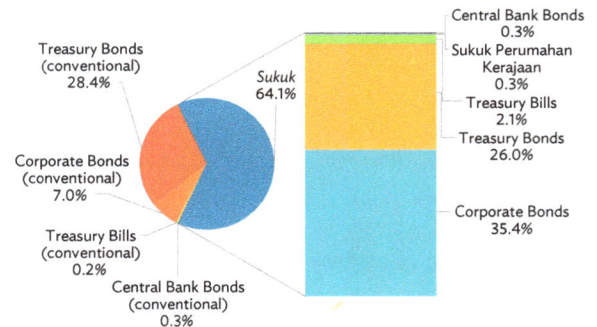

Note: Sukuk Perumahan Kerajaan are Islamic bonds issued by the Government of Malaysia to refinance funding for housing loans to government employees and to extend new housing loans.
Source: Bank Negara Malaysia Fully Automated System for Issuing/Tendering.

Capital Flows

Foreign portfolio flows into the Malaysian bond market amounted to MYR9.8 billion in Q2 2023 (Figure 5).
For the second consecutive quarter, the Malaysian market recorded net portfolio inflows. Foreign holdings of LCY government bonds rose to 23.1% of this market segment at the end of June, up from 22.7% at the end of March, due to easing consumer price inflation in Malaysia and as the yields of Malaysian fixed-income securities were relatively more attractive than those of US Treasuries.

Figure 5: Capital Flows in the Local Currency Government Bond Market in Malaysia

MYR billion

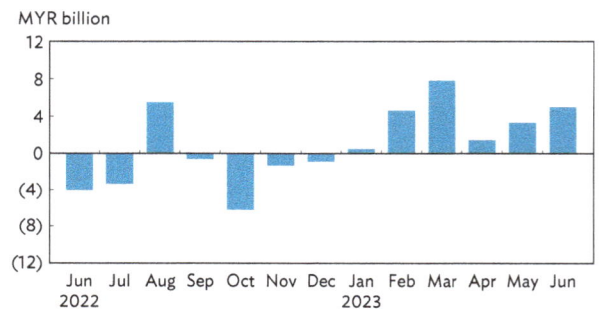

( ) = negative, MYR = Malaysian ringgit.
Notes:
1. Figures exclude foreign holdings of central bank bonds.
2. Month-on-month changes in foreign holdings of local currency government bonds were used as a proxy for bond flows.
Source: Bank Negara Malaysia Monthly Statistical Bulletin.

Philippines

Yield Movements

Local currency (LCY) government bond yields in the Philippines increased for most tenors between 1 June and 31 August (Figure 1). Only the 1-month and 3-month tenors posted declines during the review period. The increase in yields was influenced by the Bangko Sentral ng Pilipinas' hawkish tone amid persistent elevated inflation despite a continued decline since February. Consumer price inflation steadily eased to 4.7% y-o-y in July from a peak of 8.7% y-o-y in January but remains above the government's target range of 2.0%–4.0%, leading to the monetary board's decision to keep the main policy rate at 6.25% at its past three policy meetings on 18 May, 22 June, and 17 August. In addition, an increase in yields was also influenced by dampened investor sentiment due to the economy's slower-than-expected growth of 4.3% year-on-year (y-o-y) in the second quarter (Q2) of 2023, down from 6.4% y-o-y in the previous quarter.

Local Currency Bond Market Size and Issuance

In Q2 2023, total LCY bonds outstanding increased on expansions in both the corporate and government bond markets. Total LCY bonds outstanding reached PHP11.7 trillion at the end of June on growth of 1.3% quarter-on-quarter (q-o-q). Treasury and other government bonds, which account for 82.4% of the total debt stock, grew 2.3% q-o-q in Q2 2023 as issuances exceeded maturities, while central bank securities contracted 15.8% q-o-q due to a decline in issuance in Q2 2023 amid easing inflation (**Figure 2**). The corporate bond market, which accounts for 13.6% of the total debt stock, rebounded 1.2% q-o-q in Q2 2023 due to the large volume of issuances during the quarter, a reversal from the 2.2% q-o-q contraction in the first quarter of 2023. The Philippine corporate bond market remained dominated by the property, banking, and holding firms sectors, which accounted for a collective share of 81.0% of total corporate bonds outstanding at the end of Q2 2023 (**Figure 3**).

Figure 1: The Philippines' Benchmark Yield Curve— Local Currency Government Bonds

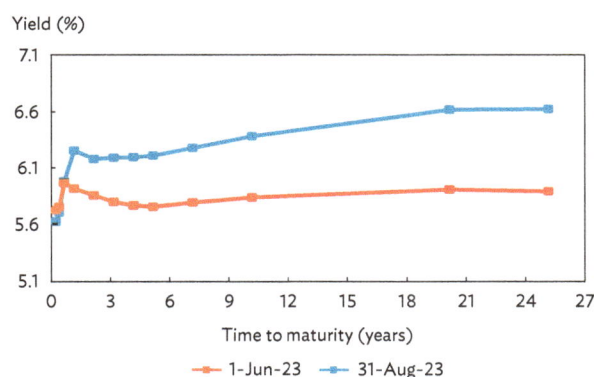

Yield (%)

x-axis: Time to maturity (years)

Legend: 1-Jun-23, 31-Aug-23

Source: Based on data from Bloomberg LP.

Figure 2: Composition of Local Currency Bonds Outstanding in the Philippines

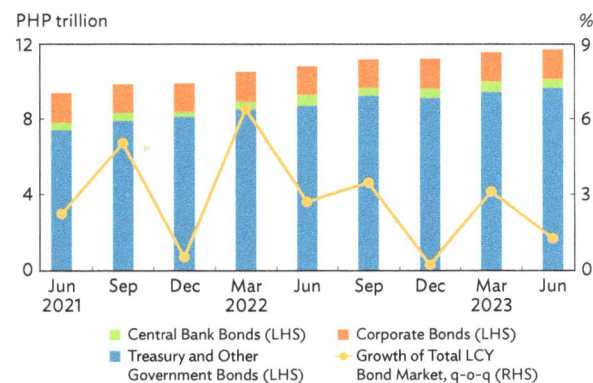

PHP trillion / %

x-axis: Jun 2021, Sep, Dec, Mar 2022, Jun, Sep, Dec, Mar 2023, Jun

Legend:
Central Bank Bonds (LHS)
Treasury and Other Government Bonds (LHS)
Corporate Bonds (LHS)
Growth of Total LCY Bond Market, q-o-q (RHS)

LCY = local currency, LHS = left-hand side, PHP = Philippine peso, q-o-q = quarter-on-quarter, RHS = right-hand side.

Note: Treasury and other government bonds comprise Treasury bonds, Treasury bills, and bonds issued by government agencies, entities, and corporations for which repayment is guaranteed by the Government of the Philippines. This includes bonds issued by Power Sector Assets and Liabilities Management and the National Food Authority, among others.

Sources: Bureau of the Treasury and Bloomberg LP.

Figure 3: Local Currency Corporate Bonds Outstanding by Sector

June 2023

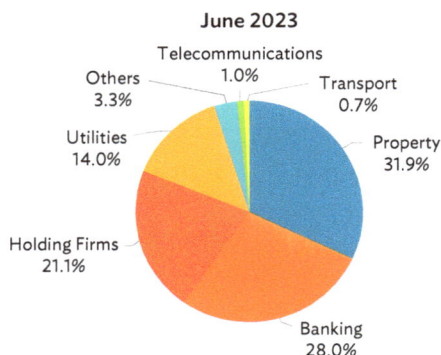

Telecommunications 1.0%
Others 3.3%
Transport 0.7%
Utilities 14.0%
Property 31.9%
Holding Firms 21.1%
Banking 28.0%

Source: Bureau of the Treasury.

Total LCY bond issuance contracted 19.2% q-o-q in Q2 2023 on reduced issuance from the government. During the quarter, a contraction of 39.0% q-o-q in the issuance of Treasury and other government bonds was mainly driven by a relatively high base in the preceding quarter brought about by the Government of the Philippines' issuance of Retail Treasury Bonds in February amounting to PHP283.7 billion (**Figure 4**). Issuance of central bank securities, which comprised 70.7% of total

issuance in Q2 2023, contracted 11.2% q-o-q as inflation continued a downtrend for six consecutive months. After a contraction of 81.7% q-o-q in the first quarter of 2023, corporate bond issuance rebounded in Q2 2023 with an expansion of 117.6% q-o-q due to a relatively low base in the previous quarter.

Investor Profile

In June 2023, the investor landscape for LCY government bonds in the Philippines was relatively the same from a year earlier as banks and investment houses continued to hold nearly half of the total LCY government debt stock. Banks and investment houses' market share climbed to 46.7% in June 2023 from 44.4% in the same period of the previous year. Contractual savings institutions and tax-exempt institutions remained the second-largest investor group in the economy's LCY government bond market, with shareholdings that decreased to 31.8% in June from 33.5% a year earlier. All other investor holdings shares remained below 10% and showed a downward trend from their previous investment percentage shares a year earlier, except for Bureau of the Treasury-managed funds, whose holdings share remained constant at around 7.0% in Q2 2023 (**Figure 5**).

Figure 4: Composition of Local Currency Bond Issuance in the Philippines

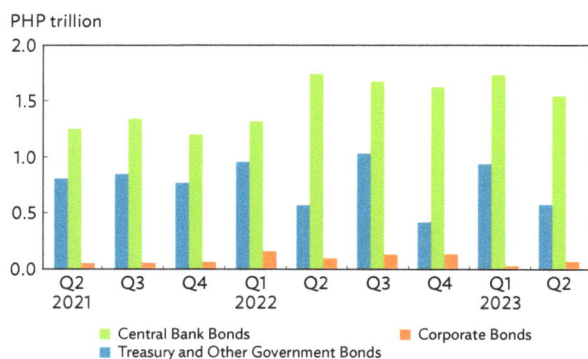

Q1 = first quarter, Q2 = second quarter, Q3 = third quarter, Q4 = fourth quarter, PHP = Philippine peso.

Note: Treasury and other government bonds comprise Treasury bonds, Treasury bills, and bonds issued by government agencies, entities, and corporations for which repayment is guaranteed by the Government of the Philippines. This includes bonds issued by Power Sector Assets and Liabilities Management and the National Food Authority, among others.

Sources: Bureau of the Treasury and Bloomberg LP.

Figure 5: Investor Profile of Local Currency Government Bonds

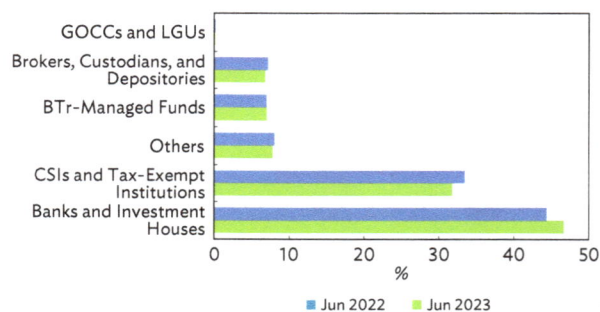

BTr = Bureau of the Treasury, CSI = contractual savings institution, GOCC = government-owned or -controlled corporation, LGU = local government unit.
Source: Bureau of the Treasury.

Singapore

Yield Movements

Singapore's local currency (LCY) government bond yields increased for most tenors between 1 June and 31 August, largely tracking the movement in the yield curve of United States (US) Treasury yields (**Figure 1**). Only the 6-month tenor posted a decline during the review period as investors opted for short-term securities amid uncertainties in the financial market. The Singapore dollar nominal effective exchange rate has been broadly stable since the Monetary Authority of Singapore (MAS)

kept its monetary policy unchanged at its last meeting on 14 April (**Figure 2**). However, US Treasury yields jumped as the US Federal Reserve raised interest rates in its July meeting to keep consumer price inflation under control while maintaining a high employment rate.

Local Currency Bond Market Size and Issuance

In the second quarter (Q2) of 2023, the LCY bond market of Singapore grew 1.7% quarter-on-quarter (q-o-q) to SGD681.9 billion. This growth was supported by higher outstanding government securities. An expansion of 3.1% q-o-q was recorded for central bank securities, extending the 4.2% q-o-q growth recorded in the first quarter of 2023. Singapore's LCY bond market was dominated by securities issued by the MAS during the review period (**Figure 3**). Growth in Singapore Government Securities bills and bonds recovered in Q2 2023, rebounding 4.4% q-o-q from a decline of 0.4% q-o-q in the prior quarter. The LCY bond market's growth, however, was dampened by the 3.8% q-o-q contraction in outstanding LCY corporate bonds due to tepid issuance during Q2 2023. Among all issuers, government-owned Housing & Development Board had the most outstanding LCY bonds, totaling SGD28.2 billion at the end of June.

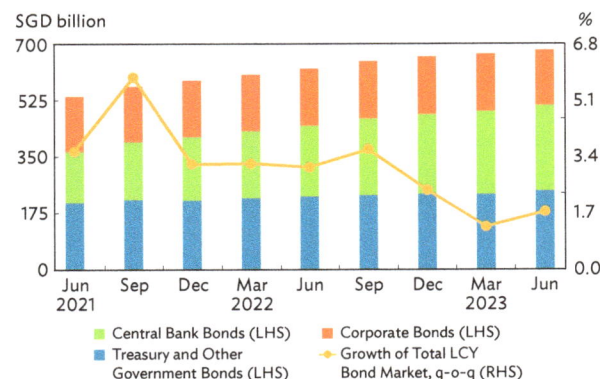

Figure 1: Singapore's Benchmark Yield Curve—Local Currency Government Bonds

Source: Based on data from Bloomberg LP.

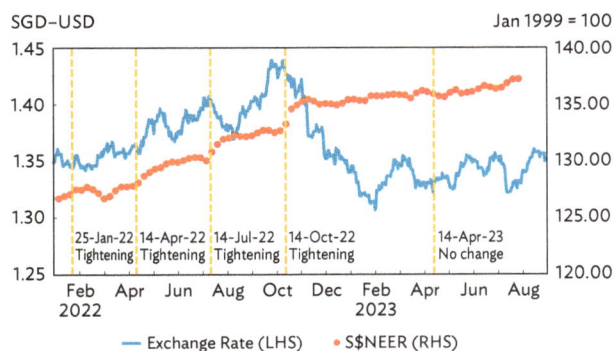

Figure 2: Exchange Rate and Monetary Policy Rates in Singapore

LHS = left-hand side, RHS = right-hand side, S$NEER = Singapore dollar nominal effective exchange rate, SGD = Singapore dollar, USD = United States dollar.
Note: Data for S$NEER are as of 28 July 2023.
Source: Monetary Authority of Singapore.

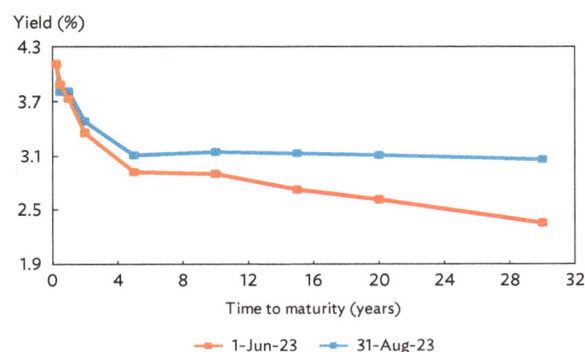

Figure 3: Composition of Local Currency Bonds Outstanding in Singapore

LCY = local currency, LHS = left-hand side, q-o-q = quarter-on-quarter, RHS = right-hand side, SGD = Singapore dollar.
Note: Corporate bonds are based on *AsianBondsOnline* estimates.
Sources: Monetary Authority of Singapore and Bloomberg LP.

Total issuance of LCY bonds in Singapore accelerated 6.9% q-o-q in Q2 2023 due to growth in issuances of LCY government securities (Figure 4). As in the preceding quarter, the majority of LCY bond issuances were from the central bank since MAS securities are regularly auctioned to manage liquidity in Singapore's financial market. A decrease of 43.9% q-o-q was recorded for LCY corporate bond issuance in Q2 2023 due to the high interest rate environment. City Developments Limited, a real estate company, raised SGD470.0 million from a 5-year bond issuance in April. The issuance was the largest corporate issue during the quarter, with the fixed-income security offering a 4.139% coupon rate. Proceeds from the issuance will be used as the company's general working capital.

Figure 4: Composition of Local Currency Bond Issuance in Singapore

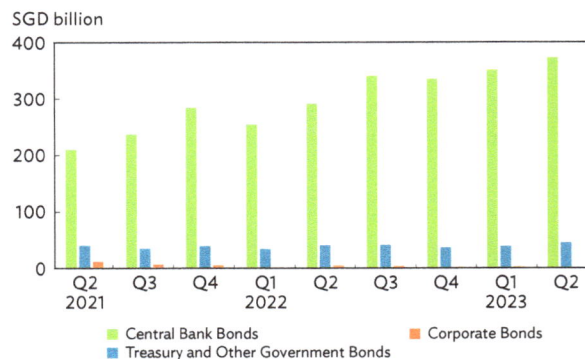

Q1 = first quarter, Q2 = second quarter, Q3 = third quarter, Q4 = fourth quarter, SGD = Singapore dollar.
Note: Corporate bonds are based on *AsianBondsOnline* estimates.
Sources: Monetary Authority of Singapore and Bloomberg LP.

Thailand

Yield Movements

Between 1 June and 31 August, Thailand's local currency (LCY) government bond yields rose for all maturities except the 20-year tenor, which fell slightly (Figure 1). The increase in bond yields was primarily driven by the Bank of Thailand's (BOT) continued monetary policy tightening. The BOT has raised its benchmark policy rate by a total of 100 basis points since January to keep inflation in check amid a sustained domestic economic recovery. Heightened risks, driven by a delay in the formation of a new government following the general election in May, also contributed to the uptick in bond yields.

Local Currency Bond Market Size and Issuance

Thailand's LCY bond market expansion moderated to 1.9% quarter-on-quarter (q-o-q) in the second quarter (Q2) of 2023. The size of the LCY bond market reached THB16.3 trillion in Q2 2023, driven by slower expansions in Treasury and other government bonds due to a relatively high volume of maturities. Treasury and other government bonds continued to dominate the Thai LCY bond market at THB9.1 trillion of bonds outstanding, representing 56.0% of total LCY bonds outstanding at the end of June (**Figure 2**). Outstanding corporate bonds (THB4.8 trillion) and BOT bonds (THB2.4 trillion) comprised 29.3% and 14.6%, respectively, of the Thai bond market.

Figure 1: Thailand's Benchmark Yield Curve—Local Currency Government Bonds

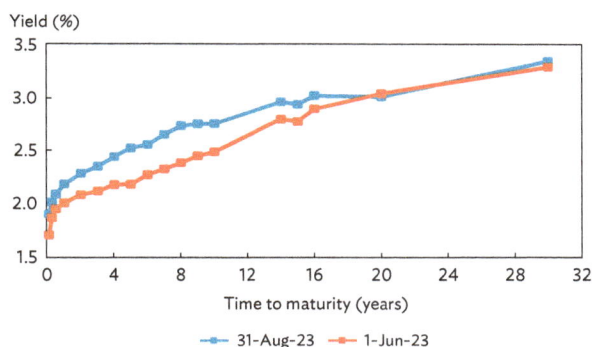

Source: Based on data from Bloomberg LP.

Figure 2: Composition of Local Currency Bonds Outstanding in Thailand

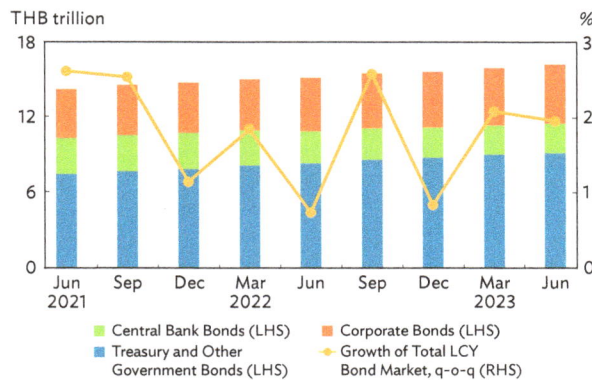

LCY = local currency, LHS = left-hand side, q-o-q = quarter-on-quarter, RHS = right-hand side, THB = Thai baht.
Source: Bank of Thailand.

Issuance of new LCY bonds accelerated to 7.1% q-o-q in Q2 2023. Total issuance of LCY bonds in Q2 2023 reached THB2.5 trillion, driven by robust issuance of Treasury and other government bonds and corporate bonds amid continued economic recovery (**Figure 3**). Treasury and other government bond issuance rose 4.1% q-o-q to THB633.5 billion in Q2 2023 following a 1.7% q-o-q contraction in the preceding quarter. Meanwhile, corporate debt issuance grew 12.0% q-o-q to THB612.7 billion in Q2 2023, as business activities gained pace amid improved economic conditions. Siam Commercial Bank was the largest corporate issuer of LCY bonds during the quarter, with total issuance of THB50.0 billion. Nonetheless, the BOT is monitoring the rollover of corporate bonds following an uptick in bond defaults. The first half of 2023 saw three corporate bonds defaults, accounting for 0.3% of corporate bonds outstanding.[6]

Investor Profile

Insurance and pensions funds and banking institutions remained the two largest investor groups in the Thai government bond market (Figure 4). Together, the two investor groups held 63.6% of total LCY government bonds at the end of June, slightly lower than their combined 66.7% share a year earlier. Foreign holdings also declined to 11.6% at the end of June from 13.2% a year prior. Meanwhile, the BOT's holdings of LCY government bonds increased from 5.0% to 6.4% during the same period. Between June 2022 and June 2023, the BOT purchased a total of THB87.5 billion of government bonds to help stabilize the bond market.

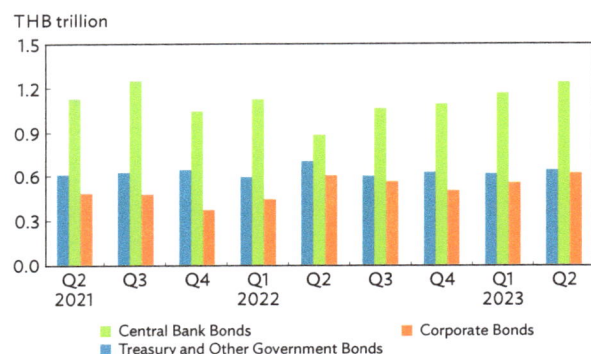

Figure 3: Composition of Local Currency Bond Issuance in Thailand

THB trillion

Q1 = first quarter, Q2 = second quarter, Q3 = third quarter, Q4 = fourth quarter, THB = Thai baht.
Source: Bank of Thailand.

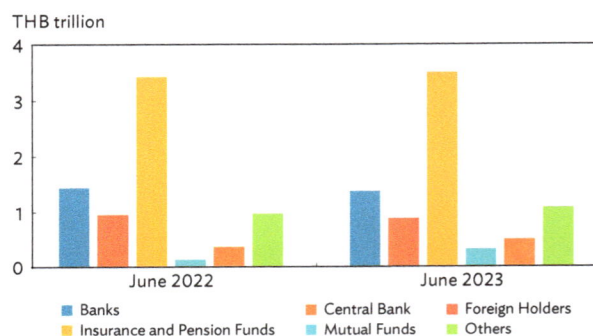

Figure 4: Investor Profile of Government Bonds in Thailand

THB trillion

THB = Thai baht.
Source: Bank of Thailand.

---

[6] *Bangkok Post.* 2023. BoT Keeps Wary Eye on Bond Rollovers. 14 August.

Viet Nam

Yield Movements

The local currency (LCY) government bond yield curve in Viet Nam shifted downward as rates declined for all tenors between 1 June and 31 August (Figure 1). Bond yields trended down as the State Bank of Vietnam continued its policy of easing and further reduced the refinancing rate to 4.50% at its policy meeting on 16 June. This followed two consecutive rate cuts in April and May, by a total of 100 basis points, to pump up its faltering economy amid easing inflation. Viet Nam's year-to-date consumer price inflation inched up to 2.0% in August from 1.1% in July but remained below the government's target of 4.5%, while its economy expanded 4.1% year-on-year in the second quarter (Q2) of 2023, accelerating from the 3.3% year-on-year growth posted in the previous quarter. Despite the faster economic growth recorded in Q2 2023, a slowdown looms as Viet Nam struggles to hit its 2023 growth target of 6.5% due to the persistent crisis in the domestic real estate industry, a slump in exports amid weak global demand, and higher lending rates that hamper business activities.

Local Currency Bond Market Size and Issuance

Outstanding LCY bonds in Viet Nam declined 4.5% quarter-on-quarter (q-o-q) in Q2 2023 due to a contraction in the corporate bond market. Corporate bonds contracted 6.6% q-o-q due to the maturation of bonds amid low issuance volume during the quarter combined with banks' increased activity in early redemptions of corporate bonds (**Figure 2**). Based on the report released by FiinRatings on 17 May, the total value of early redeemed bonds reached nearly VND11.3 trillion in April 2023. The banking sector, whose total value of early redemptions increased by 5.64 times compared to March 2023, accounted for the largest share at 61% of the total value of early redeemed bonds.

Corporate bonds outstanding reached VND688.3 trillion at the end of June, comprising 27.3% of total bonds outstanding in Q2 2023. The LCY corporate bond market in Viet Nam remained dominated by banks and property companies, accounting for 54.0% and 25.8%, respectively, of the total corporate debt stock at the end of June. There were no outstanding central bank securities at the end of Q2 2023 as the government continued to support liquidity in the economy. Meanwhile, growth in Treasury

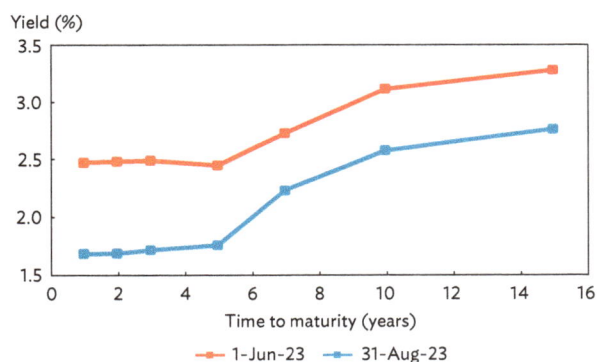

Figure 1: Viet Nam's Benchmark Yield Curve— Local Currency Government Bonds

Source: Based on data from Bloomberg LP.

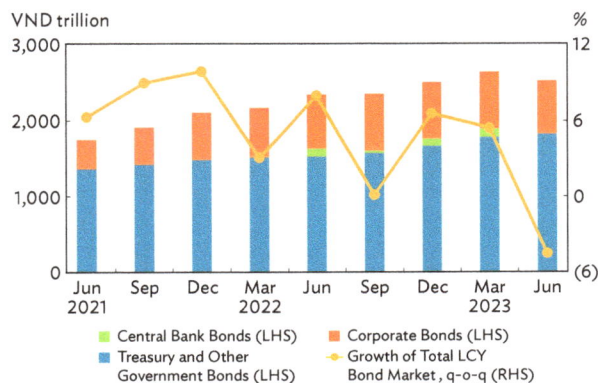

Figure 2: Composition of Local Currency Bonds Outstanding in Viet Nam

LCY = local currency, LHS = left-hand side, q-o-q = quarter-on-quarter, RHS = right-hand side, VND = Vietnamese dong.
Note: Other government bonds comprise government-guaranteed and municipal bonds.
Sources: Vietnam Bond Market Association and Bloomberg LP.

and other government bonds slowed to 2.3% q-o-q from 6.8% q-o-q in the previous quarter due to lower issuance volume in Q2 2023. Treasury and other government bonds outstanding reached VND1,830.0 trillion, accounting for 72.7% of the total debt stock at the end of June.

Viet Nam's total LCY bond issuance reached VND62.9 trillion in Q2 2023, a contraction of 93.4% q-o-q as issuances of government and corporate bonds declined during the quarter (Figure 3). Issuance of Treasury and other government bonds contracted 62.0% q-o-q during Q2 2023 to VND49.5 trillion as the State Treasury reduced its weekly auction target in June. In the same quarter, corporate bond issuance contracted 52.9% q-o-q, following sizeable issuance in March, due to negotiations in April arising from the recently enforced Decree No. 8, which allows issuers to negotiate with bondholders to restructure and extend bond payments. Despite the government's recent policy interventions, headwinds in Viet Nam's corporate bond market persist, especially for problematic real estate companies, as defaults increased to a total of VND128.5 trillion (98 issuing companies) as of 4 May, up from VND94.4 trillion (69 issuer companies) on 17 March, based on the report released by FiinRatings on 17 May. During the quarter, 13 companies issued 19 bonds totaling VND13.4 trillion, 27.9% of which were issued by firms in the property sector. Nui Phao Mining was the largest corporate bond issuer in Q2 2023, with aggregate issuance of VND2.6 trillion, followed by Construction Business Development, a company engaged in the real estate business, with issuance of a single-tranche bond amounting to VND2.3 trillion. Masan Group was the third-largest issuer of corporate bonds and had the only issuance via public offering during the quarter, with debt sales amounting to VND2.0 trillion.

Investor Profile

Insurance firms and banks remained the largest holders of LCY government bonds in Viet Nam at the end of June, together accounting for 99.5% of the total holdings (Figure 4). Insurance companies, whose investment share inched up to 58.1% in Q2 2023 from 57.8% in the previous quarter, remained the single-largest investor group at the end of June. On the other hand, bank holdings of government bonds slightly decreased to 41.4% from 41.7% in the first quarter of 2023. Among all investor groups, only banks and offshore investors posted a q-o-q decrease in their respective holdings in Q2 2023. Security companies and investment funds, as well as offshore investors, continued to hold a marginal share of less than 1.0% each at the end of June 2023.

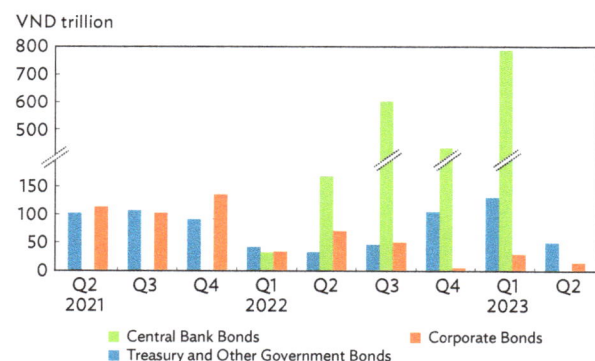

Figure 3: Composition of Local Currency Bond Issuance in Viet Nam

Q1 = first quarter, Q2 = second quarter, Q3 = third quarter, Q4 = fourth quarter, VND = Vietnamese dong.
Note: Other government bonds comprise government-guaranteed and municipal bonds.
Sources: Vietnam Bond Market Association and Bloomberg LP.

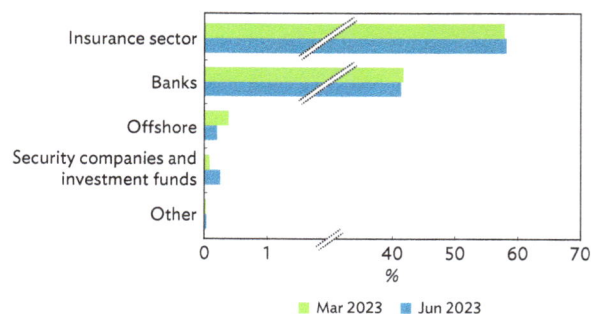

Figure 4: Investor Profile of Local Currency Government Bonds

Source: Vietnam Ministry of Finance.